I0211503

The Obscured Principles:

All You Need to Know Made Clear. Discover the Hidden Architecture of Power, Reality, and Destiny

PUBLISHED BY Thaddeus Veritas

Thaddeus Veritas

The Obscured Principles

Table of contents

Introduction...5

Chapter 1: Foundations of the Obscured: Defining Hidden
Structures 11

    1.1 Archetypal Frameworks..11

    1.2 Systemic Layers of Reality...18

    1.3 Principles of Emergence...21

Chapter 2: Power — The Unseen Mechanisms........................... 25

    2.1 Invisible Hierarchies..26

    2.2 Levers of Control 31

    2.3 Dynamics of Co-option...35

Chapter 3: Reality — Constructed Perceptions 38

    3.1 The Cognitive Matrix..38

    3.2 Media & Meme Ecology..43

    3.3 Consensus Reality...47

Chapter 4: Destiny — Patterns and Predictions........................ 51

    4.1 Pattern Recognition..52

    4.2 Probabilistic Forecasting 56

    4.3 Self-fulfilling Prophecies..59

Chapter 5: Social Networks — Invisible Webs........................... 63

    5.1 Bridges & Structural Holes 68

    5.2 Digital Amplification...72

Chapter 6: Cognitive Architectures — Mind's Blueprint............ 75

    6.1 Dual-Process Dynamics 76

    6.2 Identity & Self-Construction 81

6.3 Collective Cognition 84

Chapter 7: Symbolism — The Language of the Hidden 88

7.1 Archetypal Imagery..88

7.2 Ritual & Ceremony 94

7.3 Code Systems..97

Chapter 8: Economic Backbones — Underlying Currents......... 101

8.1 Value Extraction 106

8.2 Resource Scarcity & Allocation 109

Chapter 9: Technological Algorithms — Digital Power Grids .. 113

9.1 Network Effects & Lock-in 118

9.2 Cyber-Psychological Operations 121

Chapter 10: Synthesis — Mastering the Obscured Principles 124

10.1 Ethical Harnessing.. 129

10.2 Actionable Playbooks... 133

Conclusion 137

Introduction

"The real voyage of discovery consists not in seeking new landscapes, but in having new eyes." — *Marcel Proust*

This book is not a map. It is not a doctrine. It does not offer a singular route through the chaos of modern life, nor a panacea for its many crises. What it offers instead is a lens—a reframing of how we look at the world and, more crucially, at the unseen mechanisms that shape it. It invites the reader not to travel farther, but to perceive more deeply; not to accumulate new knowledge, but to rearrange the furniture of understanding in such a way that the familiar becomes strange, and the strange, suddenly coherent.

We live in a world profoundly influenced by forces we cannot see, rules we did not write, and systems whose logic often escapes even the most well-meaning among us. These forces operate like the hidden gears of a vast and ancient machine—always humming beneath the surface, always influencing what rises and falls, what thrives and what fails, who leads and who follows. Most people navigate this machinery blindly, mistaking symptoms for causes, distractions for direction. This book seeks to do the opposite. Its purpose is to unveil what has long been obscured: the underlying blueprints that govern power, shape human behavior, determine cultural momentum, and trace the long arc of civilizations.

This is not a collection of conspiracy theories or secret codes. Nor is it an attempt to reduce the complexity of existence into tidy laws. Rather, it is a rigorous, interdisciplinary exploration of how human systems are designed—whether consciously or unconsciously—and how they evolve. It proposes that behind every institution, every ideology, every economic structure or social trend, there exists a set of latent principles: obscured rules that exert profound influence without ever announcing themselves. These principles form what we will call the *hidden architecture* of reality.

By bringing these structures into the light, we can begin to engage with the world not merely as passive participants but as conscious co-creators of our future. Whether you are an individual seeking clarity in a noisy culture, a leader aiming to navigate complex dynamics, or a student of history trying to make sense of recurring patterns, this book offers a way to see through the fog. It offers a framework that connects psychology to politics, systems theory to spiritual inquiry, and historical precedent to future possibility. Above all, it offers new eyes.

Purpose & Scope: Revealing the Invisible Scaffolding of Civilization

Our central thesis is that behind the visible events of history, the policies of governments, and the everyday habits of people, there lie invisible frameworks that shape outcomes long before any decision is made. These are not merely sociological trends or economic laws; they are deeper patterns—what we call *obscured principles*. These include mental models, institutional logics, and structural conditions that, taken together, form the scaffolding of reality as it is experienced by individuals and societies.

We live, in many ways, within inherited paradigms—mental, cultural, and systemic operating systems—that condition how we think, feel, and act. From the unwritten norms of workplace behavior to the global movements of capital and technology, these paradigms exert influence in ways both subtle and overwhelming. The goal of this book is not only to identify and describe these patterns, but also to provide tools for navigating and, where necessary, reshaping them.

Our scope is intentionally broad, but it remains grounded. This is not an esoteric or abstract academic exercise. The obscured principles we explore are always connected to practical realities: why certain leaders gain power and others do not, why some technologies disrupt the world while others fade into obscurity, why revolutions succeed or fail, and why certain narratives persist across centuries while others vanish without a trace.

Methodology: The Fusion of Many Disciplines

To make sense of what is hidden, we must cast a wide net. No single discipline, no matter how robust, can account for the full complexity of the systems we seek to explore. Power does not operate solely through politics. Destiny is not written only in economics. Human behavior cannot be fully explained by psychology alone. Therefore, this book draws from an interdisciplinary fusion that includes:

- **Systems Theory**: To understand the dynamics of complex networks, feedback loops, emergence, and how structure influences behavior. Systems theory helps us recognize that outcomes are not always the result of individual actions, but of the configuration of the systems themselves.
- **Psychology**: To probe the cognitive biases, archetypes, and motivational drivers that shape human perception and

decision-making. At the core of every large system is the human mind—flawed, brilliant, and patterned.

- **History**: To identify recurring motifs in the rise and fall of civilizations, the transformation of institutions, and the evolution of ideologies. History provides the testing ground where obscured principles become visible in retrospect.
- **Futurism**: To speculate, with rigor, about emerging trends, technological trajectories, and the possible futures they imply. Futurism allows us to use the past and present as launchpads rather than prisons.

By weaving these perspectives together, we aim to create a coherent picture that neither reduces the world to mechanical laws nor drowns in relativism. The methodology is one of pattern recognition, synthesis, and reframing—what some might call systems-level seeing. It is not content to merely describe what is; it seeks to illuminate *why* it is, *how* it became so, and *what might emerge next*.

Key Concepts: Obscured Principles, Architecture, and Destiny

Three key concepts provide the backbone of this inquiry: **obscured principles**, **architecture**, and **destiny**. These terms are not merely poetic; they serve as organizing categories for understanding the hidden layers of reality.

1. *Obscured Principles*

These are the latent rules that shape how systems behave and how people think within them. They are often unspoken, unchallenged, and taken for granted—not because they are self-evident, but because they are deeply embedded. Examples include implicit power hierarchies, cultural myths, institutional taboos, and algorithmic biases. Obscured principles do not demand belief; they operate whether we acknowledge them or not.

We will explore how these principles govern not just macro-systems like geopolitics or global finance, but also the intimate micro-systems of identity, aspiration, and belonging. In many cases, the first step to reclaiming agency is to uncover the principle that has been governing your life without your consent.

2. Architecture

This refers to the structural frameworks that channel energy, attention, and resources. Architecture in this context is both literal and metaphorical. It includes institutional designs, economic scaffolds, media ecosystems, and even social algorithms. Good architecture is not neutral—it nudges behavior, conditions choice, and amplifies certain outcomes while minimizing others.

Much like a city planner influences human behavior through the layout of streets, these structural systems shape what seems possible, desirable, or inevitable. Our goal is to dissect these designs, to understand their affordances and constraints, and to offer insights into how different architectures could yield different destinies.

3. *Destiny*

Destiny, in the context of this book, is not a mystical preordination but an emergent trajectory. It is what happens when principles and architecture interact over time. When enough invisible patterns accumulate, when enough structural alignments are set in motion, the future begins to crystallize in predictable ways—unless interrupted by new forces or conscious interventions.

Understanding destiny as emergent allows us to approach the future with both humility and agency. We are not entirely free, but neither are we entirely bound. By mapping the trajectories already in motion, we gain the ability to anticipate and, perhaps, to alter them.

To journey through this book is to engage in a process of recalibration. Each chapter is a reframing device, a new set of lenses through which to see the world more clearly. By the end, you may not have all the answers—but you will have a map of the forces that shape answers. You will better understand why empires collapse, why social movements ignite, why myths persist, and why certain ideas come to dominate while others are buried.

You will also understand your place within these systems—not as a pawn, but as a potential architect.

This is not a book for the complacent. It is for those who sense that something is missing in the common narratives of progress, success, and power. It is for the rebels of perception, the cartographers of complexity, the quiet builders of new worlds.

Welcome to *The Obscured Principles*. Let us begin.

Chapter 1: Foundations of the Obscured: Defining Hidden Structures

"Nothing is more deceptive than an obvious fact." — Arthur Conan Doyle

We are conditioned to trust what is visible. Tangible data, explicit rules, stated objectives—these are the landmarks of modern reasoning. Yet the true engines of history, culture, and influence often lie in what is neither named nor measured. Structures do not always announce themselves; they are often embedded, recursive, and coded into language, story, and symbol. They endure because they remain largely invisible—taken for granted, assumed as natural.

Before we can decode the hidden principles that shape human reality, we must first examine the foundations on which these principles rest. The most primal of these foundations is narrative. But not just any story—*archetypal frameworks* that have traveled across time and cultures, embedding themselves into human institutions, leadership styles, brands, revolutions, and religions. These archetypes are the scaffolding beneath what seems new, the silent templates that give shape to chaos. In this chapter, we begin with these deep molds of meaning.

1.1 Archetypal Frameworks

Long before formal systems existed—before economies, governments, or organized religions—humans told stories. Around campfires, in painted caves, and through song, early communities transmitted memory, warned of danger, and offered guidance. But these stories were never purely entertainment. They were operating manuals encoded in myth, instructing how to live, how to lead, how to endure, and how to die.

What's remarkable is not merely that storytelling is universal, but that the *patterns* of these stories are nearly identical across civilizations. These repeating characters and plots are what psychologist Carl Jung and mythologist Joseph Campbell called *archetypes*—universal templates embedded in the collective unconscious, shaping how we interpret reality.

Archetypes are not specific people, but roles. They are not specific myths, but skeletal frameworks onto which cultures project their values and fears. They include the Hero, the Sage, the Trickster, the Ruler, the Outcast, and many others. These figures are not only tools of fiction—they are the invisible grammar behind movements, brands, ideologies, and institutions. In short, they are hidden structures.

The Hero, the Sage, and the Trickster: Templates of Power

The *Hero* is perhaps the most iconic archetype, and also the most manipulated. The hero's narrative is one of departure, ordeal, transformation, and return. It is a journey that begins with discomfort or disillusionment and culminates in the attainment of some boon—be it wisdom, liberation, or power. Campbell famously codified this into the "monomyth" or Hero's Journey: a cyclical structure that has shaped not only mythology but also modern cinema, politics, and corporate marketing.

The Obscured Principles

Yet behind the heroic image is a strategic function. The Hero archetype is deeply appealing because it mirrors the aspirations of the audience. A product, leader, or movement framed through the Hero lens invites identification, loyalty, and belief in transformation. Every revolution casts itself as a heroic departure from corruption. Every disruptive brand sells itself as a journey against the odds.

Then comes the *Sage*—the bearer of wisdom, the mentor, the guide. In myth, this is Merlin to Arthur, Yoda to Luke, or Chiron to Achilles. In society, the Sage shows up as the philosopher, the elder statesman, the spiritual teacher. But in modern corporate contexts, the Sage archetype is rebranded into the "thought leader," the university, the expert, or the high-end consultancy. They do not seek to transform the world directly but to provide the knowledge or tools that allow others to do so.

Unlike the Hero, the Sage represents continuity and memory. While heroes burn through the old, sages preserve it. But crucially, institutions built around the Sage must preserve their aura of insight. Universities brand themselves not merely on utility, but on tradition, genius, and authority. Think tanks position themselves as keepers of foresight. Even AI companies use the Sage motif— portraying their models as advanced minds solving problems humans can't.

And then there is the *Trickster*—perhaps the most misunderstood archetype. Loki in Norse myth, Hermes in Greek myth, or Coyote in Native American lore, the Trickster breaks rules, inverts hierarchies, and creates through destruction. Today's tricksters appear in stand-up comedians, hackers, culture jammers, and meme-makers. The Trickster reveals the absurdity of structure by mocking it, disrupting it.

Tricksters are not anarchists without purpose. They often catalyze necessary change. In the corporate world, challenger brands adopt the Trickster mold to shake up markets. Twitter users acting as whistleblowers or cultural critics play this role in politics. The function of the Trickster is not to destroy for the sake of it, but to reveal what is hidden—to make the unconscious conscious through provocation.

These archetypes—Hero, Sage, Trickster—do not operate in isolation. They coexist, compete, and hybridize within systems. A tech startup might begin as a Trickster, grow into a Hero, and then rebrand as a Sage. Political figures might adopt multiple archetypes simultaneously, depending on their audience. These are not fixed identities but narrative roles that can be adopted, discarded, and weaponized.

Cultural Convergence and the Mirror of Myth

Why do societies separated by oceans and centuries tell the same stories? Why do the epics of ancient India, West Africa, and Scandinavia all feature the wise elder, the heroic warrior, the comic disruptor?

This is not simply coincidence, nor is it cultural diffusion alone. Archetypes emerge from shared human experiences—birth, death, conflict, love, exile, return. They reflect the inner architecture of the psyche. As Jung posited, these forms arise from what he called the *collective unconscious*—a set of deep mental structures common to all people. Archetypes are not just narratives but cognitive blueprints. They help us make sense of uncertainty, assign meaning to chaos, and anticipate the behavior of others.

In practical terms, this convergence means that certain stories work *everywhere*. Hollywood knows this. So do religious missionaries, politicians, and multi-national advertisers. The reason a Marvel movie succeeds in Shanghai, São Paulo, and Berlin is not cultural sameness but mythological resonance. The journey of the Hero— facing inner and outer demons, finding allies, and returning changed—is a story that exists because it *works*. It is not only entertaining but comforting: it validates the belief that struggle leads to redemption, and that one person's change can shift the world.

But convergence also carries risk. The dominance of one mythic structure—especially when exported through global media—can erase local stories, flatten nuance, and create monocultural expectations. When every leader must be a Hero, we forget the quiet, system-building work of Sages. When every brand must "disrupt," we undervalue repair, continuity, and craft. The power of archetypes lies in their plurality—not in reducing the world to one mold, but in recognizing many.

The Monomyth in Modern Branding

Joseph Campbell's Hero's Journey was intended as a descriptive framework, but in the hands of 21st-century strategists, it became a *prescriptive tool*. Marketers, screenwriters, startup founders, and even self-help authors now use the Hero's Journey as a blueprint. The reason is clear: it works.

Let us examine Apple as a prime example. In its iconic 1984 commercial, Apple cast itself as a rebel (Trickster) shattering the conformity of IBM (the established Ruler). With the iPod and later the iPhone, Apple transitioned to a Hero narrative—"Think

Different"—inviting users to see themselves as creative protagonists, not consumers. Over time, as Apple matured and dominated, it absorbed the Sage role—offering "tools for creatives," "digital wellness," and "ecosystems of harmony." Apple, through its evolution, mastered the full archetypal cycle.

Nike follows a similar path. Its campaigns don't focus on shoes; they focus on struggle and triumph. "Just Do It" is the call to adventure. Athletes are the mythic heroes, facing adversity. Nike is the mentor, the enabler of transformation. The product is incidental—the story is everything.

Even in politics, candidates frame their campaign journeys in Heroic terms: humble beginnings, resistance from elites, dark nights of the soul, redemption through the people's trust. The monomyth is not merely branding—it becomes identity. People *live* these roles.

But this manipulation of archetypes can become hollow. When every product is a call to greatness, when every app is "revolutionizing" something, the audience becomes numb. The challenge today is not to deploy archetypes, but to *mean* them—to embody them authentically. Archetypes, when misused, become clichés. When honored, they become compasses.

Archetypes are not frozen relics of pre-modern minds. They are evolving software—running in the background of human interaction, reactivating in new forms. They shape the architecture of influence not by force, but by familiarity. They feel right, not because they are always true, but because they are ancient echoes.

To understand how systems gain legitimacy, how movements gain momentum, how brands achieve cult status, and how ideologies root themselves—one must first understand the archetypal frameworks they inhabit. These frameworks are not optional extras; they are structural codes.

In the chapters to come, we will expand beyond narrative into economics, institutions, and emergent behaviors. But none of it can be fully understood without this foundation. Before there are laws, there are stories. Before there is policy, there is myth. Before we build, we dream—and we dream in archetypes.

1.2 Systemic Layers of Reality

To understand the obscured principles that shape our world, it is not enough to look at events in isolation or people as independent actors. We must instead perceive society as a layered system—each stratum interacting with and influencing the others, often in subtle and recursive ways. Reality, as experienced by individuals and societies, is structured like a multi-tiered operating system. It is not built on a single plane of causality, but upon interwoven realms that include the physical, informational, and symbolic. Each layer has its own logic, yet none exists independently. Together, they create the complex matrix within which power operates, behavior emerges, and meaning is constructed.

The **physical layer** is the most visible and seemingly concrete. It includes the tangible structures of civilization—cities, roads, transportation networks, supply chains, satellites, electrical grids, factories, and all the material scaffolding that supports human life. These are the engineered systems that create the substrate for interaction. The global shipping network, for example, is not merely a technical accomplishment; it is a geopolitical structure that determines the price of goods, the vulnerability of nations, and the rhythm of daily life. A delay in one node—a port closed due to weather or strike—can cascade across economies. Likewise, the shape of a city, its zoning policies, the placement of highways and rail lines, all function as silent architectures that govern behavior. They decide who has access to opportunity and who does not, what flourishes and what withers.

But the physical alone cannot explain our world. Over it lies the **informational layer**—a rapidly evolving realm of data, signals, and synthetic intelligence. This is the domain of media, software, and algorithms: the nervous system of contemporary civilization. Unlike the physical, this layer is weightless, invisible, but no less potent. It determines what we see, how we communicate, and what we come to believe. Algorithms curate our social feeds, prioritize certain news, censor other content, and silently shape the cognitive terrain in which decisions are made. A viral video can start revolutions, a deepfake can destroy reputations, and a few lines of code can crash markets. While the physical world moves in industrial rhythms, the informational layer pulses in milliseconds.

This layer is also recursive; it feeds back into the physical. Consider the gig economy: platforms like Uber or Amazon Flex use data flows to orchestrate real-world logistics, matching drivers to passengers or products to homes. The infrastructure is still concrete—cars, warehouses, roads—but the coordination is digital. The informational layer overlays the physical like a digital exoskeleton, bending it to new efficiencies and vulnerabilities.

Beneath both of these, and in many ways above them, is the **symbolic layer**—perhaps the most foundational of all, though often the least acknowledged. This is the realm of meaning: myths, rituals, ideologies, cultural narratives, moral codes, and value systems. It is here that the justification for all systems is either granted or denied. A bridge may span a river, a server farm may store a nation's data, but it is the symbolic that tells us *why* they matter, *what* they represent, and *who* benefits. It is the symbolic that convinces soldiers to die for flags, consumers to buy for brands, and citizens to comply with laws written on paper.

The symbolic layer does not require physicality; a nation, a religion, a currency—all are symbolic structures supported by shared belief. The U.S. dollar, for instance, is not backed by gold but by faith in the system that issues and defends it. The same holds true for constitutions, contracts, and marriages. These are not natural facts, but symbolic constructs—made real by collective adherence. Symbols organize emotions and perceptions. They bind individuals into groups, create in-group/out-group distinctions, and encode values into rituals and traditions.

What becomes fascinating—and critical—is the interplay between these layers. A disruption in one often reverberates through the others. The fall of the Berlin Wall was a physical event, but it marked the collapse of a symbolic order and triggered a new informational narrative about the "end of history." A blackout caused by an overburdened grid may begin as a physical failure, but quickly becomes an informational crisis (miscommunication, panic, misinformation) and eventually a symbolic wound (loss of trust in governance or institutions). Likewise, a symbolic shift—such as the rise of environmental consciousness—can transform the informational layer (new narratives, new metrics) and ultimately reshape the physical (transition to green energy infrastructures).

Understanding reality as layered allows us to identify leverage points more precisely. Some problems cannot be solved at the physical layer alone; they require narrative shifts. Others are not merely "messaging" issues but need structural, infrastructural change. Recognizing the interdependence of the physical, informational, and symbolic is essential for decoding modern complexity—and for designing better systems in the future.

1.3 Principles of Emergence

While layered systems give us a map of where power and influence reside, they do not explain *how* complexity arises. For that, we must turn to the concept of *emergence*—the process by which local interactions produce global order. Emergence is one of the most powerful yet underappreciated principles governing both natural and artificial systems. It allows us to understand how decentralized actions can give rise to coherent structures, why small changes can lead to massive shifts, and how stability or chaos unfolds through feedback loops.

At its core, emergence is about *pattern without design*. No single ant decides the structure of the colony, and yet the colony operates with breathtaking efficiency. There is no central brain coordinating the movements of a murmuration of starlings, yet their flight appears choreographed. These systems are bottom-up, not top-down. Intelligence is distributed, not centralized. It is from the micro-interactions—simple rules repeated at scale—that macro-level order arises.

In human systems, we see the same logic. The structure of a language, the formation of social norms, the flow of traffic, or the volatility of markets—these all emerge from countless small choices, none of which are sufficient on their own to explain the whole. Decentralized finance (DeFi), for example, operates without traditional banking institutions. It is based on smart contracts and peer-to-peer transactions that, when aggregated, form robust financial ecosystems. No one governs DeFi in the traditional sense, yet it functions, adapts, and even innovates.

Emergence also helps explain sudden, dramatic transformations. These are often described as **tipping points** or **phase transitions**—moments when a system, pushed just beyond a critical threshold, shifts into a new state. Water becomes steam not gradually, but all at once. A society tolerating minor injustices may suddenly erupt in revolution when a single event catalyzes accumulated tensions. These are nonlinear dynamics. They defy prediction through simple extrapolation. The challenge is that tipping points are usually visible only in hindsight. Yet by studying systems closely—especially their feedback structures—we can begin to identify early-warning signals.

The **feedback loop** is the mechanism that often determines whether a system trends toward stability or chaos. **Positive feedback loops** amplify change. In financial markets, a sudden drop in price may cause panic selling, which causes further drops, triggering more panic. This is the logic of contagion, both in biology and information. Viral posts on social media become more visible the more they're shared, creating echo chambers where extreme views dominate. Left unchecked, positive feedback loops can lead to runaway effects—market crashes, riots, or technological bubbles.

In contrast, **negative feedback loops** stabilize systems by dampening deviation. A thermostat is a classic example: when the temperature rises, the cooling system activates, restoring balance. In ecosystems, predator-prey dynamics often self-regulate population sizes. In human systems, regulations, norms, and institutional checks can serve as negative feedback mechanisms—if they're functioning properly. The challenge in modern societies is that many traditional dampeners have weakened, while amplifiers have grown exponentially—especially in the digital realm.

The Obscured Principles

Emergence is not inherently good or bad. It is simply a pattern of complexity. It can produce beautiful order (as in ant colonies or cultural renaissances) or terrifying breakdown (as in mob violence or financial collapse). Its outcomes depend on the *rules at the local level*—what agents are optimizing for, how information flows, and what constraints or freedoms exist. A society that prioritizes short-term gain, rewards echo chambers, and removes stabilizing institutions is structurally predisposed to volatility.

Yet emergence also offers hope. It suggests that change need not wait for top-down permission. Small actions, if patterned correctly, can scale. Norms can shift through culture, not just policy. Innovation can arise from the edge, not just the center. But to harness emergence, we must understand it. We must become literate in its dynamics.

The great task, then, is to design systems—social, technological, economic—that are *emergence-aware*. This means thinking in terms of feedback loops, thresholds, incentives, and local behaviors. It means moving beyond command-and-control models to architectures that facilitate healthy self-organization. In such systems, leadership is not about dictating every outcome, but about shaping the conditions under which desirable patterns emerge.

As we proceed through this book, emergence will return again and again—not as a theory, but as a living principle embedded in everything from civilization collapse to AI development. The obscured principles we seek to uncover often emerge *themselves*— not written in manifestos, but revealed through behavior at scale. The goal is not to master emergence as if it were a machine, but to recognize its pulse—to know when to intervene, when to step back, and when to redesign the rules at the root.

Understanding emergence is understanding destiny in motion. It is the invisible current beneath events, the silent architect of outcomes. It is not a force to be feared or worshiped—but to be studied, respected, and, when possible, ethically engaged.

Chapter 2: Power — The Unseen Mechanisms

Fact: Only 4% of decision-makers control over 90% of global wealth.

Power, in its most effective form, is not what is declared, but what is denied—denied visibility, denied access, and denied scrutiny. It does not always dress in robes or uniforms. It does not always sit on thrones or hold office. Power that endures does so by disappearing from the frame while continuing to shape the scene. It embeds itself in norms, in architectures, in the patterns that govern decisions long before any vote is cast or deal is signed. This chapter explores the anatomy of such power—not the symbols, but the mechanisms. Not the illusion of control, but the system of control itself.

To understand how the world is truly run, one must learn to look beyond headlines, beyond election cycles, and beyond the stagecraft of governance. One must learn to decode the invisible hierarchies—those networks, alliances, and leverage points that organize influence without ever making their presence explicit. The irony is profound: in an age of transparency, where we are inundated with information, real power increasingly resides where light cannot reach.

2.1 Invisible Hierarchies

At first glance, power appears to be structured through formal hierarchies—governments, corporate boards, legal systems, bureaucracies. These are the visible pyramids: presidents, CEOs, judges, generals. Their roles are codified, their duties published, their titles clear. These individuals and institutions are the faces of authority, and in many cases, they wield genuine influence. But to stop there is to mistake the theater for the script. Beneath every official organ lies an unofficial anatomy—*informal power structures* that not only support the formal, but often guide it from the shadows.

A government may be run by ministers and parliaments, but behind these actors are unelected advisors, think tanks, lobbyists, donors, and media operatives. A corporation may list its executive leadership, but major decisions often come from behind closed doors—via private equity groups, venture capitalists, or legacy shareholders. These backchannels—consulting dinners, undisclosed memos, informal alliances—are not accidents. They are features of the system, not bugs. They allow flexibility, plausible deniability, and above all, insulation from public accountability.

The distinction between formal and informal power is not merely theoretical—it is architectural. Formal structures are what the public sees; they are mapped, monitored, and often regulated. Informal structures are what actually *move* the levers. In times of crisis or transition, it is often the informal networks that ensure continuity. For instance, during political upheavals, financial institutions, intelligence agencies, or industrial lobbies may maintain influence regardless of which party wins. What is popularly called "the deep state" is in many ways an informal continuity structure—

those actors who outlast political tides and act as custodians of long-term strategic interests.

This brings us to the notion of **shadow networks**—interconnected webs of individuals and institutions that operate outside official charts but have disproportionate influence. These networks can be composed of billionaire philanthropists funding ideological projects through foundations, multinational law firms crafting transnational legal loopholes, or intelligence agencies collaborating across borders without democratic oversight. They are not conspiracies in the cinematic sense; they are ecosystems of mutual interest, built on access, discretion, and shared incentives.

One of the most effective tactics of shadow networks is fragmentation. Influence is never centralized in one room or one person; it is distributed across roles, jurisdictions, and intermediaries. This fragmentation creates deniability. A tech company may avoid antitrust scrutiny by routing its operations through dozens of subsidiaries. A political lobby may influence legislation not through direct payments, but through think tanks, sponsored research, or "independent" consultants. Each actor can claim neutrality, even as they serve a common purpose.

Consider the role of elite conferences like Davos or Bilderberg. These are not legislative bodies, nor do they produce binding agreements. But they are hubs—points of convergence where leaders from finance, politics, media, and academia meet, align narratives, and shape agendas. What is said on stage may be banal; what happens in side meetings is where consensus is crafted. The value of these gatherings is not in publicity, but in proximity.

To map such influence, we must abandon the traditional org chart. We must instead think in terms of *network analysis*—a tool borrowed from systems theory and sociology. Network analysis allows us to visualize and quantify relationships between actors. It reveals not just who holds what title, but who interacts with whom, how frequently, and under what contexts. A junior staffer who serves as a gatekeeper for a major decision-maker may wield more power than a titled director. A hedge fund manager who sits on multiple nonprofit boards, donates to political campaigns, and has personal ties with media executives may be a silent architect of public perception.

The technique involves mapping nodes (individuals or institutions) and the edges (the relationships between them). Centrality measures can then be used to identify key influencers—not necessarily the most visible, but the most connected. This method has revealed surprising insights in fields ranging from criminal networks to innovation clusters. Applied to politics or global finance, it shows that influence often bypasses formal lines and flows instead through affinity, access, and embedded trust.

Another approach is **stakeholder mapping**—a strategic method used in organizational management and conflict resolution to identify all parties with a stake in a particular issue. In the context of hidden power, stakeholder mapping expands beyond the obvious. It includes silent partners, regulatory bodies, activist groups, and even algorithmic systems. In a content moderation dispute, for example, stakeholders may include the platform's trust & safety team, advertisers, civil rights organizations, user communities, and policymakers—each with leverage over outcomes, none with total control.

We must also consider the **timing of influence**. Power is not always about issuing commands; sometimes it's about shaping the preconditions under which others make decisions. If you can define the problem, set the agenda, or determine the default options, you do not need to control the final vote. This is the principle behind *choice architecture*—popularized in behavioral economics—but also behind legislative framing and media narratives. Those who shape the discourse early often win long before the public even notices a debate has begun.

Importantly, invisible hierarchies are not static. They evolve. As new technologies emerge, as geopolitical balances shift, as social norms transform, the composition and methods of influence adapt. The rise of social media, for instance, created new power centers: influencers, digital activists, decentralized autonomous organizations. But even these emergent powers are being subsumed into older hierarchies. Platforms originally hailed as democratizing forces are now battlegrounds of algorithmic manipulation, with influence concentrated in the hands of a few executives, engineers, and opaque AI models. The gatekeepers may have changed, but the gates remain.

Understanding invisible hierarchies is not merely a diagnostic exercise; it has profound implications for democracy, justice, and agency. If decisions are being made beyond public scrutiny, if accountability is diluted across layers of influence, then formal institutions risk becoming hollow. Elections may continue, policies may be debated, but the direction of society will be set elsewhere—offstage, by hands unseen.

The challenge, then, is how to engage with these realities without falling into cynicism or paralysis. Awareness is the first step. By learning to read between organizational charts and beyond press releases, we begin to see the real architecture of influence. From there, the task is to redesign systems that reward transparency, that distribute power more equitably, and that create feedback loops between formal authority and informal impact.

The rest of this chapter will delve deeper into the mechanisms of influence—how soft power operates, how narratives are seeded, how systems are captured, and how consent is manufactured. But for now, let this truth stand: real power is not always where it seems. It hides in trust networks, in unrecorded meetings, in shared ideologies and inherited access. To perceive it requires not just new tools, but new eyes.

And once you see it, you cannot unsee it.

2.2 Levers of Control

Control is not always imposed through brute force or authoritarian decree. In sophisticated systems, domination is rarely overt. It wears the face of consensus, appears as common sense, and moves silently through institutions. The most effective forms of control do not feel like coercion; they feel like choice. Beneath this illusion of freedom lies a matrix of levers that those in power deploy to guide perception, gate access, and shape behavior. These levers are not always operated with malice or conspiracy—they are often mechanisms that have evolved to preserve stability and maintain predictability. But they carry costs, especially when they concentrate power without accountability. Among these, three stand out: asymmetries of information, control over key resources, and the subtle but potent psychological levers that guide human motivation.

Information asymmetry is one of the most fundamental tools of modern control. When some actors have access to critical knowledge that others do not, they are able to shape outcomes without ever needing to impose their will directly. In the political arena, this plays out through media framing. The same event, depending on how it is reported, can become a scandal, a hero's journey, or a footnote. The framing determines public reaction more than the event itself. Language becomes a battlefield— "enhanced interrogation" instead of torture, "collateral damage" instead of civilian death, "disruption" instead of exploitation.

This framing is not accidental. It is the product of editorial decisions, institutional biases, and economic incentives. News organizations, even when they claim neutrality, operate within ecosystems funded by advertising, constrained by access to sources, and shaped by audience expectations. More dangerously, in an age of algorithmically optimized content, visibility itself becomes a commodity. Stories that align with dominant narratives rise to the top, while dissenting voices struggle to gain traction. Control over information is no longer merely about censorship; it is about *selection*. What is *not* covered, what is *not* emphasized, what is *allowed* to fade quietly—these are the new instruments of shaping reality.

Information asymmetry extends far beyond media. In markets, investors with access to private data or insider knowledge consistently outperform those operating on public signals. In technology, platforms harvest vast quantities of user data, refine behavioral models, and use them to optimize engagement or manipulate choices, all while users remain unaware of the extent of surveillance. The asymmetry is structural—those who collect, interpret, and act on information faster and more completely hold an immense advantage. They can predict, influence, and often preempt dissent.

Another central lever is the control of resources—particularly capital, land, and technology. These are the substrates upon which modern life is built, and those who gate their distribution wield disproportionate influence. Access to funding determines what projects are possible, what startups get built, what research gets published, and even what political campaigns are viable. Venture capital, private equity, philanthropic foundations—these are the financiers of the future, shaping not only markets but also moral discourse.

Land, though often treated as a legacy asset, remains a cornerstone of power. It dictates who controls food production, who profits from real estate, and who gets displaced by gentrification or development. Ownership patterns are deeply unequal, and land accumulation continues to function as both a hedge against volatility and a vector of control. Those without land or secure housing live in a perpetual state of vulnerability, often priced out of agency.

Technology, meanwhile, has become the new infrastructure of domination. From communication networks to artificial intelligence, those who control digital platforms do not merely own tools—they own *channels of attention*. A handful of companies dictate the flow of billions of conversations daily. Their decisions about content moderation, monetization, and feature design affect political outcomes, mental health, and economic mobility. They are not governments, yet they govern.

The final set of levers are psychological. Unlike physical force or legal coercion, psychological influence works through emotional induction. It leverages fear, desire, shame, pride, and a host of other primal impulses. Fear is perhaps the oldest and most reliable tool. Fear of the outsider, the unknown, the loss of security—these emotions are repeatedly weaponized to justify repression, surveillance, and conformity. When people are afraid, they seek authority. They crave order. In times of crisis, extraordinary powers are often granted—and rarely returned.

Desire, too, is a potent inducement. The promise of wealth, beauty, fame, success—these are used to lure compliance and internalize norms. Advertising doesn't merely sell products; it sells identities. It conditions people to associate consumption with worth, to measure self against impossible ideals, and to seek belonging through acquisition. Entire populations are trained to desire what they are told to need, thus becoming complicit in their own control.

This form of inducement creates what philosopher Byung-Chul Han calls the "achievement society," where individuals believe they are free agents pursuing personal goals, even as they exhaust themselves in systems that extract value from every action. Control, in this model, is no longer external pressure but internalized compulsion. People surveil themselves, optimize themselves, and punish themselves for failing to meet standards they did not choose.

The genius of these levers lies in their invisibility. They rarely provoke revolt because they do not feel like oppression. They operate through consensus, aspiration, and the silent conditioning of environments. By the time people realize the extent of their influence, the architecture is already built, and resistance feels futile.

But these mechanisms are not immutable. What is constructed can be deconstructed. The challenge is to cultivate awareness—not just of what controls us, but how. Once the levers are seen, they can be resisted, redesigned, or reimagined. But first, they must be named.

2.3 Dynamics of Co-option

Power does not always crush what threatens it. Often, it absorbs. The most enduring systems of control are those that learn to adapt, not by attacking resistance directly, but by *co-opting* it. They take the symbols of rebellion, drain them of disruptive content, and repackage them in palatable forms. Dissent becomes merchandise. Radical voices become spokespeople. Movements become marketing campaigns. This process—co-option—is one of the most effective and least understood dynamics of modern governance.

Cultural appropriation is the most obvious and historically persistent form of co-option. Dominant groups adopt the aesthetics, language, or rituals of marginalized communities, often stripping them of their original context and politicized meaning. What begins as a symbol of resistance—a hairstyle, a rhythm, a garment—becomes a trend. Once a cultural artifact is detached from its roots, it can be commodified, sold, and neutralized. The original meaning is blurred or erased, and the act of appropriation is rebranded as appreciation or innovation.

But co-option goes beyond culture. It operates at the level of ideas. Radical critiques of capitalism, for instance, are often defanged by integrating their language into corporate branding. Words like "disruption," "empowerment," "sustainability," and "authenticity" are routinely deployed in marketing campaigns that preserve the very systems those terms once critiqued. Environmentalism is repackaged as greenwashing. Social justice is turned into PR slogans. The presence of activist language gives the illusion of change, while insulating existing hierarchies from substantive transformation.

Thaddeus Veritas

One of the more insidious forms of co-option is the formation of *strategic alliances*—in which challengers to the status quo are invited into the system under the guise of inclusion. Activists are given advisory roles. Independent journalists are offered corporate partnerships. Nonprofits receive funding from the very industries they are supposed to critique. In some cases, this is well-intentioned. In others, it is calculated.

The mechanism works through proximity. Once inside the system, the outsider must navigate institutional pressures: maintaining access, protecting reputation, avoiding alienation. The revolutionary edge dulls. Compromises are made. Narratives are softened. Over time, the distinction between the critic and the institution blurs. The challenger is no longer an adversary, but a stakeholder.

Co-option can also be observed in the lifecycle of revolutions. History shows that few revolutions remain radical after their initial rupture. The cycle often unfolds in three phases: eruption, institutionalization, and normalization. In the eruption phase, grievances accumulate, a catalyst ignites them, and established structures are overwhelmed. This is the moment of rupture—when the old order cracks.

But chaos is unsustainable. In the institutionalization phase, the revolution solidifies into new structures: parties, laws, doctrines, bureaucracies. These are necessary for stability, but they come at a cost. The fervor of the original moment is replaced by rules, gatekeepers, and compromise. In time, the new regime begins to resemble the one it replaced. Symbols change, but systems persist.

Normalization is the final phase. The revolutionary ideals are archived, memorialized, and often romanticized. They are taught as history, not praxis. What was once radical becomes conventional. New elites emerge. Dissent is reabsorbed. The cycle closes, and the machinery resumes.

This is not to say that revolutions are futile. They shift the coordinates of what is possible. They rupture the illusion of inevitability. But their energy is finite, and systems are resilient. Co-option is not a betrayal of revolution—it is the method by which power survives revolutions.

To resist co-option, awareness is not enough. It requires structural imagination. Can we build movements that are resistant to absorption? Can we create institutions that regenerate critique rather than suppress it? Can we preserve the tension between transformation and stability without collapsing into either cynicism or authoritarianism?

The answer may lie in designing systems that are open but not vulnerable—flexible enough to adapt, yet principled enough to resist dilution. This requires not just strategy, but a revaluation of success. If movements measure themselves by mainstream acceptance, they risk becoming the next status quo. If they define success as preserving integrity, they must also embrace the risk of marginalization.

Co-option is inevitable in systems that reward conformity. But so is resistance. The task is not to escape the cycle, but to interrupt it—again and again—with clarity, creativity, and courage. Only then does transformation stand a chance of remaining true to itself.

Chapter 3: Reality — Constructed Perceptions

Statistic: 90% of brain activity is subconscious processing.

Reality, as most people understand it, is a fragile agreement—a negotiated illusion that arises not from objective facts, but from interpretations filtered through neurological patterning, emotional associations, and social consensus. What we call "real" is often the result of countless invisible filters—most of them operating below the threshold of conscious awareness. Though we imagine ourselves as rational beings navigating a stable world, the truth is more unsettling: our experience of reality is less a direct perception than a simulated construction assembled by the brain in real time.

This chapter begins by exploring the mechanisms through which the human mind interprets the world. If 90% of brain activity occurs beneath consciousness, then the majority of what we believe, feel, and decide is being processed beyond our reach. From this fact emerges a foundational insight: we do not perceive reality as it is, but as our minds are conditioned to see it. The result is a kind of cognitive matrix—a web of shortcuts, stories, and illusions that shape every dimension of human experience.

3.1 The Cognitive Matrix

The brain is not a mirror; it is a sculptor. Faced with an overwhelming influx of sensory input—light, sound, texture, motion, emotion—it cannot process everything in raw form. Evolution solved this problem through efficiency. Rather than

The Obscured Principles

analyze every new situation from scratch, the brain developed shortcuts: heuristics, pattern-recognition systems, and probabilistic models that allow for rapid decision-making. These shortcuts work most of the time, and they are what allow us to function in a complex world. But they also come at a price. What we gain in speed, we often lose in accuracy.

One of the most pervasive forms of mental shortcutting is the use of **heuristics**—simple rules of thumb that reduce cognitive load. These include availability heuristics (judging the likelihood of an event based on how easily examples come to mind), representativeness heuristics (assuming something belongs to a category based on resemblance), and anchoring (relying too heavily on the first piece of information encountered). These mental tools are not flaws; they are features of an adaptive mind. But they can lead us astray, particularly in environments saturated with manipulation.

Biases are the emotional cousins of heuristics. They are less about efficiency and more about predisposition. Confirmation bias, for instance, causes us to seek out and interpret information in ways that affirm our existing beliefs. Cognitive dissonance makes us uncomfortable with contradictory evidence, often leading to its dismissal. The backfire effect—the tendency for people to strengthen their beliefs when presented with contradictory evidence—shows how tightly narratives bind to identity. Over time, these biases harden into blind spots, narrowing our ability to see clearly even as we grow more confident in our understanding.

Yet perception is shaped by more than individual cognition. The human mind does not float freely; it is anchored in story. From a young age, people learn to organize reality through **narrative architecture**. Stories are not merely entertainment; they are

39

cognitive scaffolding. They give events meaning, characters purpose, and experiences coherence. A story has a beginning, a middle, and an end. It identifies heroes and villains. It provides causal logic where life often offers only randomness.

This narrative impulse is both a gift and a vulnerability. It allows humans to transmit complex knowledge across generations—morals, histories, identities—but it also tempts them to impose order where there is none. When a plane crashes, we seek a villain. When a disease spreads, we search for a story that explains why. This desire for narrative closure can lead to scapegoating, conspiracy thinking, or overconfidence in simplistic solutions. Political ideologies, religious doctrines, and even scientific paradigms function as competing meta-narratives, offering different explanatory models for the same phenomena.

In modern media ecosystems, narrative is weaponized. A news headline does not merely report a fact; it activates a schema. A viral tweet doesn't just share an event; it cues an emotional response and invites identification with a tribe. Entire information economies are now structured around storytelling—the faster, more dramatic, and more emotionally resonant the story, the more attention it captures. In this way, narratives become currencies of influence. They are not evaluated for truth so much as for coherence and alignment with audience expectation.

Beyond cognition and narrative, there is the world of **illusion**—not in the mystical sense, but in the very tangible ways our senses deceive us. Optical illusions, for instance, reveal how vision is not passive reception but active interpretation. The brain fills in gaps, adjusts contrasts, and interprets spatial relationships based on context. This is why static images can appear to move, why colors shift depending on adjacent hues, why perspective tricks can warp size perception. The mind does not record the world like a camera; it reconstructs it like an editor.

But the more profound illusions are **social and interpretative**. Social illusions occur when group consensus overrides individual judgment. This is the domain of the Asch conformity experiments, where participants gave obviously incorrect answers to fit in with a group. It's also the realm of mass hysteria, moral panics, and echo chambers. People see what others see. Or more precisely, they believe they see what others *claim* to see. Reality becomes a collective hallucination, sustained by mutual reinforcement.

Interpretative illusions arise from framing—how questions are posed, how problems are defined, how contexts are shaped. A policy described as a "tax cut" activates a different response than the same policy described as a "revenue loss." A refugee can be described as a "threat" or a "survivor," changing the moral register entirely. These shifts in language are not semantic games; they alter neural pathways, emotional responses, and ultimately, political behavior.

At the heart of these illusions is a simple truth: perception is not truth. It is a rendering. And renderings can be hacked.

This has led to what some theorists call the "reality crisis" of the 21st century—not just a crisis of facts, but of trust in the *mechanisms* by which facts are verified. Deepfakes, AI-generated texts, fake news, ideological bubbles—these are not anomalies. They are the logical outcomes of a system where perception is malleable, and control over perception equals control over belief. In such a system, to manipulate how people *feel* about reality is more powerful than to shape reality itself.

Yet amid this complexity, there is opportunity. To understand the cognitive matrix is not to despair, but to become literate in perception. It is to recognize that while we cannot escape bias, we can *map* it. While we cannot stop narratives, we can *analyze* them. While we cannot prevent illusion, we can *contextualize* it.

Education becomes not just the transfer of knowledge, but the training of awareness. Media literacy is not optional—it is foundational. Philosophical humility, emotional regulation, and interdisciplinary curiosity become survival tools in a world where clarity is increasingly rare.

Ultimately, the human mind is not just a passive receiver of reality—it is a co-author. To become conscious of the ways we construct the world is the first step toward reimagining it. The illusion is not that reality is unreal, but that our access to it is ever complete.

What we must seek, then, is not perfect perception, but *conscious construction*. Not absolute truth, but honest engagement with complexity. In this way, the cognitive matrix can become less a prison and more a map—a tool not only for understanding what is, but for imagining what could be.

3.2 Media & Meme Ecology

The modern mind no longer navigates a stable landscape of information. Instead, it swims in a turbulent, constantly shifting media ecology where truth competes not with lies, but with noise, distraction, and distortion. The boundaries between fact, fiction, satire, and manipulation have blurred—not simply because bad actors push disinformation, but because the very structure of digital communication rewards virality over accuracy, emotion over depth, and spectacle over reflection. This media ecosystem is not neutral. It is a living, evolving environment, shaped by algorithms, sustained by attention, and populated by memes—units of cultural transmission that propagate like biological genes.

Memetics, once a speculative metaphor, has in the internet age become an observable phenomenon. The idea that ideas themselves evolve through replication, mutation, and selection helps explain how certain phrases, images, beliefs, and behaviors spread with the force of epidemics. A meme, in its original sense as defined by Richard Dawkins, is not just a joke captioned on a picture—it is any cultural unit capable of replication: a slogan, a trend, a narrative frame, a catchphrase, a political dog whistle. What gives memes their potency is not just repetition, but resonance. The more a meme fits existing cognitive patterns—fears, hopes, identities—the more likely it is to be shared, internalized, and defended.

In traditional societies, memetic transmission was slow. Ideas passed through oral storytelling, rituals, and formal institutions. Today, the speed is exponential. Platforms like TikTok, Twitter, Reddit, and YouTube function as viral breeding grounds, where attention functions as currency and shareability is the mark of survival. In this environment, ideas are optimized not for truth but for transmissibility. A simple, emotionally charged meme can outcompete nuanced analysis. Humor, outrage, and aesthetic novelty enhance memetic fitness, while accuracy becomes secondary or irrelevant.

The structure of digital communication has supercharged this process through **algorithmic curation**. Content is no longer encountered in linear formats or through shared cultural reference points. Instead, every user is presented with a tailored feed—an ever-adapting mirror that reflects their preferences, biases, and behavior back at them. These algorithms, designed to maximize engagement, inadvertently produce **filter bubbles** and **echo chambers**. Within these self-reinforcing loops, individuals are exposed mostly to information that confirms their worldview, and rarely to dissenting voices or contradictory evidence.

This phenomenon is not just technological; it is psychological. The brain seeks cognitive consistency. We are more comfortable when what we see aligns with what we believe. Algorithms exploit this bias by feeding us content that flatters our assumptions, makes us feel seen, or triggers outrage toward out-groups. Over time, the divergence between informational ecosystems deepens. Two people can inhabit the same physical space but live in entirely different perceptual realities. Political polarization, cultural fragmentation, and the erosion of shared narratives are symptoms of this deeper structural condition.

But the dangers of the media ecology do not end with fragmentation. Within this architecture emerge more weaponized forms of manipulation: **disinformation vectors** that deliberately distort, deceive, or disrupt. These vectors include everything from deepfakes—synthetic media generated by artificial intelligence that simulate real people saying or doing things they never did—to coordinated propaganda campaigns operated by state and non-state actors. Disinformation today is not a matter of clumsy forgeries or obvious lies. It is sophisticated, plausible, and often couched in half-truths.

Propaganda bots—automated accounts that amplify certain messages, hijack hashtags, or harass dissenting voices—are used to simulate consensus and manipulate visibility. Troll farms, whether ideological or profit-driven, flood comment sections, derail conversations, and spread memes engineered to provoke. Sometimes, disinformation is not intended to persuade but simply to confuse. The goal is not to make people believe something false, but to make them doubt whether *anything* can be true. In this strategy—often referred to as "firehose of falsehood"—volume replaces clarity. Trust in media erodes. People retreat further into their tribal silos or give up altogether.

The media ecology has also become the terrain of soft power. Nations, corporations, influencers, and movements all engage in memetic warfare. The most successful campaigns do not feel like propaganda; they feel like entertainment, authenticity, or community. The ability to shape the narrative—what is talked about, how it is framed, what becomes emotionally salient—has become more valuable than the capacity to enforce policy. Narrative dominance precedes legal or military dominance. The meme becomes the prelude to the regime.

Yet despite its volatility, this media environment is not entirely nihilistic. Memes can also carry truth, mobilize resistance, and foster awareness. Whistleblower leaks, viral social justice campaigns, and movements like #MeToo or Arab Spring all relied on the speed and scale of memetic transmission. The problem is not memes themselves, but the lack of media literacy in the public and the lack of transparency in the platforms that curate them.

To navigate the meme ecology is to recognize its rules. Not everything that spreads is important. Not everything that trends is true. Influence is no longer signaled by position or expertise, but by visibility. The architecture of attention is the architecture of power. The question is no longer *who speaks*, but *who is heard*—and under what conditions.

Understanding memetics, algorithmic curation, and disinformation is essential for anyone seeking to reclaim agency in the construction of meaning. Reality, as mediated by screens, is not discovered—it is designed. And those who design the flow of memes are shaping not just opinion, but perception itself.

3.3 Consensus Reality

If perception is the individual lens, and media the environment in which it is shaped, then **consensus reality** is the collective hallucination we agree to inhabit. It is the shared framework of assumptions, stories, values, and symbols that bind a society into coherence. We do not all see the world the same way, but we see it similarly enough to coordinate, legislate, and remember. This shared reality is not natural; it is negotiated, revised, and, at times, imposed. To understand consensus reality is to examine how beliefs spread, stabilize, and, sometimes, collapse.

One of the most powerful forces in shaping consensus is **social proof**—the psychological mechanism by which individuals infer truth or legitimacy based on the behavior of others. When people are uncertain, they look to the group. If everyone is running in one direction, we assume there must be danger. If everyone believes a politician is corrupt, or a product is superior, or a practice is shameful, we tend to align ourselves accordingly. This dynamic is not a weakness of rationality; it is a feature of evolutionary intelligence. Social proof helped early humans survive in uncertain environments. But in the modern world, it becomes a tool of mass suggestion.

Social media platforms supercharge social proof. Likes, retweets, shares, view counts, and trending tags all serve as signals of collective endorsement. These metrics do not just reflect opinion— they *create* it. Something becomes "true" not because it has been verified, but because it is widely accepted. The bandwagon effect reinforces dominant narratives and marginalizes dissent. Ideas that receive traction early often snowball, not because they are more valid, but because they gain first-mover visibility. Consensus becomes self-reinforcing.

However, consensus requires not only peer validation but **institutional validation**. Institutions—academia, religious authorities, governments, scientific bodies—have traditionally functioned as anchors of epistemic authority. They stabilize the discourse by providing official interpretations, definitions, and archives of meaning. When NASA announces a discovery, or a court delivers a verdict, or a university issues a study, the weight of institutional legitimacy transforms belief into accepted knowledge.

Yet this mechanism is fragile. Institutional trust is built over time but can unravel quickly. Scandals, politicization, economic capture, or epistemic failures can erode public confidence. When institutions are perceived as biased, corrupt, or opaque, their pronouncements no longer bind consensus. The result is epistemic fragmentation— where each group turns to its own trusted validators, and shared reality fractures into competing "truth markets."

Nowhere is this process more evident than in the case study of **public opinion on climate change**. For decades, climate science was institutionally grounded, with broad consensus among scientists about anthropogenic global warming. Yet public belief lagged, and in many cases, regressed. Why?

The answer lies in the interplay of media framing, social proof, and institutional trust. Early on, fossil fuel interests funded campaigns to sow doubt, using the language of scientific skepticism to suggest uncertainty. Media outlets, seeking "balance," often gave equal time to climate deniers and climatologists, creating a false equivalence. The result was not outright disbelief, but confusion. If the experts can't agree, how can we?

The Obscured Principles

Social proof further complicated the picture. In communities where climate denial was widespread, individuals who questioned it risked ostracization. Conversely, in more liberal circles, concern about climate became a marker of identity. The debate was no longer about data—it was about belonging.

Eventually, a cultural shift occurred. Activist movements like Fridays for Future and Extinction Rebellion, celebrity endorsements, and a series of devastating climate events shifted the emotional valence of the issue. Climate concern became mainstream, even fashionable. Institutional messages remained largely unchanged—but perception finally aligned.

This demonstrates a core feature of consensus reality: *truth is necessary, but not sufficient.* For a belief to become dominant, it must pass through cultural, emotional, and social filters. Institutions provide the scaffolding, but people build meaning through interaction. The failure to recognize this dynamic explains why many factual campaigns fail to change minds. They offer information, but not story; evidence, but not trust.

In the end, consensus reality is a collaborative construction. It emerges from the tension between authority and belief, fact and feeling, signal and noise. It can be manipulated, but also rebuilt. It can be fragile, but also regenerative. What is required is not blind conformity, nor cynical relativism, but a deeper literacy in how beliefs form, spread, and harden.

To live in a pluralistic society is to negotiate overlapping realities. But without some shared terrain, dialogue becomes impossible. Consensus is not agreement on everything—it is agreement on enough. It is a working fiction we use to build roads, draft laws, tell histories, and plan for futures.

Thaddeus Veritas

And like any fiction, it must be authored with care.

Chapter 4: Destiny — Patterns and Predictions

"Prediction is very difficult, especially about the future." — *Niels Bohr*

The desire to foresee what lies ahead has haunted humanity since its earliest days. From the casting of bones and the reading of stars to economic forecasts and climate models, our species has never stopped trying to peer around the corner of time. Yet as the Danish physicist Niels Bohr noted, prediction is no easy task—particularly when it involves systems as complex, chaotic, and reflexive as societies, economies, or the human mind itself. Still, while absolute certainty remains elusive, patterns do not. History whispers in recurring rhythms. Systems echo previous configurations. Crises, though often presented as novel, often emerge from familiar trajectories. The study of these repetitions and signals is not superstition—it is strategic foresight.

To speak of destiny in this context is not to invoke fate, but to acknowledge structure. Destiny, as we mean it here, is not predetermination but the arc that emerges when certain conditions persist, when feedback loops harden, and when collective choices solidify into trajectories. These trajectories are not fixed, but they are directional. And by recognizing the early contours of change, we can begin to anticipate not just what is likely to happen, but what may be possible to redirect.

4.1 Pattern Recognition

To forecast the future, one must first listen to the past. Not to memorize it, but to read it as a living archive of behavioral loops, institutional rhythms, and civilizational thermodynamics. The most enduring attempts at systemic foresight have been built upon the observation that human societies tend to oscillate. Empires rise and fall. Economies expand and contract. Social cohesion gives way to fracture, which in turn births new orders. The specific expressions may differ, but the motion often rhymes.

Among the most famous frameworks for understanding these historical patterns is the theory of **Kondratiev waves**, proposed by the Russian economist Nikolai Kondratiev in the early 20th century. He argued that capitalist economies move in long-term cycles of boom and bust—lasting approximately 40 to 60 years—driven not just by financial markets but by major technological innovations. These waves, he suggested, unfold in four seasons: prosperity, recession, depression, and recovery. The steam engine, railroads, electricity, and the internet each sparked their own wave, altering the fabric of production and reshaping global relations.

While controversial and sometimes contested, Kondratiev's framework remains influential because it aligns with observable long-term shifts. For instance, the digital revolution of the 1990s and 2000s did not merely alter communication—it restructured labor markets, financial systems, and social behavior. As that wave matures, many argue we are entering a new transition, driven by artificial intelligence, biotechnologies, and planetary constraints. Recognizing the phase of a wave can help institutions prepare—not by preventing downturns, but by understanding their causes and crafting resilient responses.

The Obscured Principles

Parallel to economic waves are **generational cycles**, most famously articulated in the Strauss-Howe generational theory. According to this model, societies cycle through four generational archetypes in roughly 80- to 100-year periods, with each archetype reacting to the conditions left by its predecessors. These cycles—comprising a "high," "awakening," "unraveling," and "crisis"—suggest that major historical events (like wars or societal overhauls) tend to recur when societies reach a critical point of institutional decay and generational tension. While not deterministic, this model draws attention to the rhythms of cultural renewal and generational psychology.

But historical models are not enough. We live in an age of acceleration, where change no longer unfolds at the pace of decades but of days. In this context, pattern recognition must evolve. One of the most powerful tools at our disposal is **data mining**—the practice of extracting meaningful patterns from vast and seemingly unstructured digital information. Today, billions of tweets, purchases, search queries, supply chain fluctuations, and biometric records offer unprecedented insight into real-time human behavior. This isn't merely about surveillance; it is about sensing weak signals before they become dominant trends.

A single viral tweet may not mean much—but the emergence of a new meme, repeated across geographies and demographics, may signal a shifting cultural undercurrent. A sudden increase in Google searches about economic anxiety, or a spike in food shortages along global supply chains, may foreshadow political unrest. The data itself is not the story; it is the texture from which stories emerge. When analyzed at scale, patterns begin to form. Clusters of sentiment, waves of interest, tremors of panic—all appear first as noise, but coalesce into signal if one knows how to listen.

Corporations and governments already invest heavily in such analysis. Hedge funds track shipping data to anticipate commodity shortages. Intelligence agencies monitor encrypted chatter for signs of insurgency. Social media platforms observe behavioral shifts not only to sell ads, but to predict the next political movement or viral trend. Increasingly, the future is not imagined—it is modeled. But modeling has its limits. Data without context becomes misleading. Anomalies may be random, or they may be early signals of a phase shift. The challenge lies in interpretation.

This is where **early-warning indicators** come into play. These are not predictions in the conventional sense, but threshold markers— signs that a system is approaching a point of transformation. In ecology, this may include rapid species loss or biodiversity collapse. In economics, it might be credit bubbles or sharp increases in debt-to-income ratios. In politics, it may involve institutional gridlock, declining trust in media, or surges in populist rhetoric.

The goal is to identify not just when a system is in crisis, but *when it becomes vulnerable* to crisis. These indicators are often subtle: changes in migration patterns, shifts in birth rates, the emergence of new slang among youth populations, disruptions in niche commodity markets. By the time a crisis becomes obvious, it is often too late to influence its direction. True foresight depends on detecting the tremors, not waiting for the quake.

One example is the Arab Spring. On the surface, the revolutions seemed spontaneous. But data analysts later observed a rising wave of online dissent, economic grievances, and demographic pressures months—even years—before the first protest erupted. The signals were there: unemployment spikes, food inflation, censorship battles, youth frustration. What was missing was synthesis—a framework to connect the dots before the moment of ignition.

The Obscured Principles

In a more recent context, the COVID-19 pandemic illustrated both the potential and the limits of early-warning systems. Researchers and journalists flagged the novel coronavirus weeks before it became a global emergency. But institutional inertia, political denial, and fragmented communication delayed response. The data was clear. The pattern was visible. What failed was the coordination to act on it.

Thus, pattern recognition is not merely a technical skill; it is a cultural and institutional challenge. It requires humility to accept that models may be flawed, but also the courage to act before certainty arrives. It requires interdisciplinary synthesis—combining history, economics, behavioral science, systems theory, and intuition. And most of all, it requires a deep awareness of the biases that blind us to emerging realities.

Humans are conditioned to favor stability. We resist acknowledging inflection points until they are undeniable. We anchor to the recent past, assuming tomorrow will resemble yesterday. But systems do not always bend gradually. Sometimes they break. Sometimes they leap.

The task of recognizing patterns is therefore not simply to predict. It is to prepare. It is to spot the inflection points where intervention is still possible. It is to understand that the future is not a place we arrive at, but one we shape—consciously or not—through attention, adaptation, and action.

Destiny, then, is not a prophecy. It is a field of probabilities, shaped by currents both visible and obscured. To see its shape emerging through the fog is not to know its outcome, but to gain agency within it. And that, in an uncertain world, may be the most powerful knowledge of all.

4.2 Probabilistic Forecasting

In a world of accelerating complexity and cascading interdependencies, the demand for clarity about the future grows ever louder. Governments, institutions, corporations, and individuals alike seek tools to make sense of what's coming. Yet the very nature of the systems we attempt to forecast resists tidy prediction. Linear cause-and-effect models break down in the face of feedback loops, emergent properties, and nonlinear transitions. In such a landscape, the practice of forecasting must evolve beyond single-outcome prediction toward something more robust, adaptable, and honest: probabilistic thinking.

Probabilistic forecasting acknowledges a crucial truth: the future is not fixed. It is not a destination waiting to be discovered but a constantly shifting field of possibilities shaped by countless interacting variables. Within this field, some futures are more likely than others, but none are guaranteed. The task, then, is not to forecast *what will happen*, but to map the *likelihood* of different scenarios, and to update these maps as new evidence emerges.

Scenario planning is one of the most pragmatic approaches to this mindset. Developed originally by military strategists and refined by corporations during times of uncertainty, scenario planning does not attempt to divine a single correct future. Instead, it constructs multiple plausible narratives based on combinations of known variables and key uncertainties. Each scenario becomes a testing ground for decisions. How would our strategy perform if geopolitical alliances shifted? What would happen if a new technology disrupted our industry sooner than expected? What if extreme weather events became routine?

Importantly, scenario planning is not speculation for its own sake. Its value lies in exposing blind spots and in preparing minds and institutions to act with agility rather than paralysis. When leaders rehearse a range of potential futures—optimistic, pessimistic, and ambiguous—they reduce the shock of surprise. They cultivate resilience by asking, "What would we do *if?*" rather than clinging to "This *will* happen." By making room for uncertainty, scenario planning paradoxically increases clarity.

The ability to move fluidly between probabilities is further enhanced by a mindset rooted in **Bayesian thinking**. Named after the 18th-century mathematician Thomas Bayes, this approach is not a forecasting model in itself, but a method for continuously updating beliefs based on new information. At its core lies a simple principle: when presented with fresh evidence, revise your assumptions.

In Bayesian logic, one begins with a prior belief—a baseline estimate based on existing knowledge. When new data becomes available, this belief is adjusted upward or downward depending on how strongly the evidence supports or contradicts it. This process avoids the binary trap of "true vs. false" and replaces it with an evolving scale of probability. Beliefs become dynamic, not dogmatic.

Applied practically, Bayesian reasoning is transformative. Consider a pandemic. Early on, data may be scarce and uncertain. A Bayesian forecaster begins with cautious priors based on similar past outbreaks. As infection rates rise, mutation patterns emerge, and vaccine developments progress, these priors are refined. Rather than anchoring on initial assumptions or swinging wildly with each headline, Bayesian forecasters remain tethered to a logic of continual recalibration.

This thinking is especially vital in the face of **black swan events**— unforeseen disruptions that are low in probability but extreme in impact. Popularized by Nassim Nicholas Taleb, the term "black swan" refers to those events that lie outside normal expectations, that carry massive consequences, and that are often rationalized in hindsight as if they were predictable. The 2008 financial crash, the COVID-19 pandemic, and the fall of the Soviet Union all fit this pattern.

Black swan events challenge traditional forecasting precisely because they defy trend lines. They emerge from the fat tails of statistical distributions—those areas usually dismissed as noise or anomalies. But in complex systems, it is often the rare event that redefines the system entirely. These events remind us that risk is not the same as uncertainty. Risk can be measured; uncertainty cannot. And yet, black swans do not render forecasting useless. They invite us to build systems that are not optimized for efficiency alone but designed for adaptability and shock absorption.

In this light, probabilistic forecasting becomes not just a technical exercise but an ethical stance. It asks us to hold our convictions lightly, to update our models without ego, and to design strategies that survive surprise. It pushes back against false precision, against the seduction of definitive pronouncements, and instead embraces a posture of preparation.

To forecast probabilistically is to admit that we cannot eliminate uncertainty—but we can learn to navigate it with more wisdom, humility, and foresight.

4.3 Self-fulfilling Prophecies

While probabilistic forecasting attempts to describe the future as a range of possibilities, it must also contend with a paradox: sometimes, merely *believing* in a particular future can bring it into being. This phenomenon is known as the **self-fulfilling prophecy**, and it is among the most powerful yet underexamined forces shaping human history. At the intersection of belief, behavior, and outcome, self-fulfilling prophecies reveal that the future is not only something we predict—it is something we co-create.

The classic example is a bank run. If enough people believe a bank is about to collapse, they will withdraw their funds en masse. That collective behavior, driven by anticipation rather than fact, leads to the very collapse that was feared. The prophecy becomes true *because* it was believed. Markets operate on similar reflexivity. Expectations of inflation can drive inflation. Confidence in a startup can drive its valuation sky-high, while doubt—even unfounded—can cause its sudden death.

This feedback between belief and outcome is not confined to economics. It pervades education, politics, relationships, and social systems. A teacher who expects a student to succeed may, unconsciously, provide more encouragement and attention, leading the student to rise to that expectation. A society that expects its youth to become violent may treat them with suspicion and hostility, reinforcing alienation and leading to the very violence feared.

Such dynamics show that anticipation is not passive. It acts on the world. Anticipation directs energy, attention, resources, and behavior. When structured over time, it becomes what sociologist

Robert Merton called "ritualized expectations"—collective beliefs that become embedded into systems, policies, and institutions. These expectations do not merely reflect the world; they help shape it.

Consider the role of economic forecasts in national budgets. If a government believes a recession is imminent, it may cut spending or raise interest rates. These moves, while intended as preemptive safeguards, may inadvertently depress demand and trigger the recession they sought to prevent. On the other hand, overconfidence can lead to bubbles, where the collective exuberance for an asset—be it real estate, cryptocurrency, or tulips—disconnects from fundamentals. The story fuels the price, and the price justifies the story, until the illusion breaks.

In politics, the effects are equally profound. A narrative of inevitable decline can demobilize populations, suppress civic engagement, and erode social trust. A narrative of progress can galvanize innovation, collaboration, and resilience—even if the underlying conditions are difficult. This is not a question of delusion, but of framing. The stories societies tell about their trajectory influence how people act within them.

This feedback loop between story and structure has led thinkers to describe the modern age as one dominated not by ideology, but by **narrative warfare**. Competing visions of the future—some apocalyptic, others utopian—compete for dominance. Each narrative seeks not only to describe reality but to recruit believers whose actions will make that reality more likely.

In this context, **managing narrative** becomes a strategic act. It is not merely public relations or propaganda—it is about shaping the anticipatory horizon. Corporations do it when they promise "the future of mobility" or "a better tomorrow." Political campaigns do it when they project hope or fear. Social movements do it when they claim that "another world is possible." These are not idle slogans. They are blueprints for self-fulfilling prophecies.

However, there is danger here too. Narratives, once internalized, can become dogmas. The desire to see a particular future fulfilled can lead to confirmation bias, denial of contradictory evidence, and the suppression of dissent. A society convinced of its own moral arc may overlook structural injustices. A movement certain of collapse may reject opportunities for repair. When prophecy becomes ideology, it ceases to serve awareness and begins to shape reality blindly.

To harness the power of self-fulfilling prophecy wisely, one must cultivate both imagination and discipline. Imagination to envision futures worth living in. Discipline to distinguish between aspirational framing and delusional detachment. The narratives we choose must be rooted enough to inspire action, but open enough to allow correction.

This balance is especially crucial when confronting global challenges. Climate change, for instance, has long been framed in apocalyptic terms, which, while accurate in warning, can also produce paralysis. But shifting the narrative to one of transformation—of adaptation, innovation, and systemic reimagining—can galvanize action. The crisis remains, but the anticipation becomes constructive rather than fatalistic.

Ultimately, the future is not only about what happens. It is about what we expect, how we prepare, and what we are willing to believe is possible. A self-fulfilling prophecy, like a myth, is a story with consequences. And in a world shaped increasingly by shared belief, these stories matter more than ever.

To manage narrative is to manage destiny. Not by coercion, but by care. Not by certainty, but by conscious shaping of collective imagination. The stories we tell ourselves—and each other—will echo in the structures we build, the policies we support, the lives we choose to lead. And in that echo, the future begins to take form.

Chapter 5: Social Networks — Invisible Webs

Statistic: 70% of interpersonal influence occurs within clusters of 3–5 people.

Despite the sprawling nature of digital communication and the illusion of limitless reach, true influence remains deeply local. Not geographically, but socially. It thrives within small clusters of trust and intimacy, where credibility is not earned through credentials but through consistency, where loyalty trumps visibility, and where decisions are made not in the open marketplace of ideas, but in the quiet confidence of shared experience. Social networks are not merely technological; they are human architectures—interwoven webs of belief, perception, and loyalty. And at the heart of these webs lie micro-communities: the dense, often invisible constellations of three to five individuals that serve as the emotional, cognitive, and behavioral anchors of our lives.

To understand how influence truly spreads—not just in theory, but in practice—we must begin at this smallest unit of cohesion. These micro-communities—whether they take the form of cliques, pods, study circles, creative teams, or activist cells—are the gravitational centers around which larger cultural forces orbit. While mass media and viral content appear to drive opinion, closer examination reveals a more nuanced reality. Most people do not change their minds because of a trending hashtag or an expert's declaration; they change their minds because someone they trust said, "This made me think of you," or "We should try this," or simply, "I believe in this." Influence, in other words, is relational before it is informational.

These tightly bound social units function with an internal logic. Trust is not abstract—it is earned through interaction, through the fulfillment of unspoken expectations, and through the history of mutual reinforcement. Within a micro-community, individuals are not just friends or colleagues; they are validators of each other's reality. What is considered plausible, acceptable, or valuable within that circle gains a weight far greater than the same idea offered from outside. This is why grassroots movements, start-up teams, and underground art scenes often begin with very small numbers yet exert disproportionate influence. When trust is high and feedback is rapid, action becomes coordinated and resilient.

Within these nodes, a kind of **trust economy** emerges. This is not tracked through digital reputational scores or formal reviews, but through a lived calculus: who shows up, who delivers, who listens, who follows through. In high-trust micro-communities, reputation operates like an informal currency. It determines whose ideas are considered, whose doubts carry weight, and whose suggestions become action. This unspoken economy influences everything from the books people read to the protests they attend, the diets they adopt to the technologies they embrace.

Importantly, the economy of trust is not transactional in the traditional sense. It cannot be bought or scaled quickly. It must be cultivated slowly, through time, reciprocity, and vulnerability. It is fragile, yet once established, it becomes the gateway through which new behaviors, values, and ideas pass. This is why external interventions—be they advertising campaigns, policy mandates, or corporate rebranding efforts—often fail when they attempt to leapfrog trust and go straight to influence. Without buy-in from trusted intermediaries within these tight-knit groups, messages bounce off or are reinterpreted through existing group norms.

This has profound implications for how we understand cultural transmission. The diffusion of innovation model, popularized by Everett Rogers, suggests that ideas spread from innovators to early adopters, then to the majority. But what this model often misses is the *social texture* of adoption. Innovations do not spread uniformly across a population; they spread through social clusters. The decision to adopt rarely happens in isolation. It is negotiated within peer groups, discussed over dinners, examined in group chats, and tested within the safe boundaries of shared perception.

The most successful ideas—be they political, artistic, technological, or spiritual—are not those with the broadest reach at launch, but those that ignite *locally* within a micro-community that has disproportionate downstream influence. This is what marketers call identifying the "right node," but in practice, it means finding those individuals who sit at the intersection of high trust and high connectivity. These people are not always the loudest or the most visible. They are often the ones who others turn to before making a decision, the ones who curate what their circles read, watch, and believe.

Seeding an idea at the right node within a micro-community is not about manipulation; it is about resonance. The idea must already contain the values, language, and aspirations of the community. It must feel organic, not imposed. When this happens, the idea does not spread *through* the group—it spreads *as* the group. It becomes part of their collective identity.

Viral ignition, then, is less about force and more about *fit*. An idea introduced too early, or in the wrong social context, will not take hold. But the same idea, introduced at the right moment, through the right person, within a trusted cluster, can cascade. This is especially true in environments saturated with information. In such contexts, people do not lack input; they lack *filters* they trust. Micro-communities serve as those filters. They help individuals decide not just *what* to believe, but *how much* to care.

This principle has been exploited, intentionally or not, by movements across the ideological spectrum. Political campaigns increasingly rely on micro-targeting strategies that attempt to replicate the dynamics of trusted small groups. Social movements, particularly decentralized ones, often replicate through peer-to-peer validation rather than top-down directives. Even misinformation campaigns now recognize that seeding a narrative in the right chat group or subreddit can have far greater impact than broadcasting it through mass media.

At the same time, micro-communities are not immune to distortion. When groupthink sets in, when dissent is punished, when the need for cohesion overrides the pursuit of truth, these clusters can become incubators of extremism, misinformation, or rigidity. What begins as a high-trust environment can become a closed loop, reinforcing false beliefs and resisting correction. The very intimacy that allows for deep influence can also create blind spots.

Yet when functioning well, micro-communities are among the most powerful engines of human growth, resilience, and transformation. They provide the safety required for vulnerability, the friction needed for clarity, and the encouragement necessary for risk-taking. They are not perfect, but they are profoundly human.

In an age where influence is often equated with reach, it is crucial to remember that change often begins small—whispered between three friends, tested in a private group, passed along in coded references. The web of social life is not flat; it is patterned with hidden knots of gravity. These knots—these micro-communities— are where real power lies. Not in the mass, but in the mesh.

To shape culture, to ignite transformation, to plant the seeds of new paradigms, one must start not with the crowd, but with the cluster. Not with the shout, but with the shared glance, the trusted voice, the inner circle. Influence, it turns out, is not always about scale. It's about depth. And in the invisible webs we weave daily, the future quietly begins.

5.1 Bridges & Structural Holes

In any social network, influence and innovation do not only depend on the density of relationships within small groups. They also depend on the links that connect those groups to one another. While micro-communities shape the emotional and cognitive worlds of individuals, it is often the bridges between these groups—the seemingly casual acquaintances, the unexpected connections—that act as the true arteries of transformation. These points of linkage are not merely decorative. They are essential to the diffusion of ideas, resources, and opportunities across the broader fabric of society.

The sociologist Mark Granovetter famously articulated this insight in his theory of the "strength of weak ties." Contrary to common assumption, Granovetter showed that our closest relationships—those with family members, best friends, and long-time collaborators—are not always the most useful when it comes to accessing new information or opportunities. Instead, it is the weaker, more casual connections—acquaintances, former colleagues, friends of friends—who often serve as the conduits to novel environments and unfamiliar insights. These weak ties act as bridges between different social clusters, allowing knowledge and influence to travel across boundaries that would otherwise remain closed.

Imagine two dense social circles: a group of musicians in a jazz collective and a team of biotech researchers in a startup. Within each circle, information circulates quickly, but tends to reinforce what the group already knows. A weak tie between a member of the jazz group and a researcher in biotech—perhaps an old college friendship—suddenly creates a channel through which unexpected connections can form: a conversation about rhythm becomes an analogy for protein folding, or a recording technique inspires a new method of data compression. These are not hypothetical musings. Cross-domain breakthroughs often begin precisely at these unanticipated intersections.

But weak ties alone are not enough. In every network, there exist **structural holes**—gaps between otherwise disconnected groups. These holes are not accidents; they are patterns. Some clusters simply do not communicate. Their values diverge, their vocabularies don't align, or their institutional incentives pull them apart. Yet within these silences lie vast potential. Those who learn to bridge structural holes—individuals who maintain ties across different worlds—occupy uniquely powerful positions. They are not necessarily the most central or visible figures in a network, but they are often the most pivotal.

These individuals are known as **brokers** or **gatekeepers**. Their power lies not in producing ideas, but in **translating** and **transferring** them. The broker sees what one group takes for granted and recognizes its novelty in another context. They do not merely pass information along; they adapt it, reframe it, make it legible to a different audience. A broker might introduce a startup's innovation to a government agency, or connect a community activist to an academic institution. Their function is catalytic. Without them, systems remain fragmented. With them, the flow of insight becomes fluid, and new coalitions become possible.

Yet brokerage is a delicate position. With great access comes the temptation to control the flow of information for personal gain. Gatekeepers, especially within hierarchical or bureaucratic systems, can obstruct progress as easily as they can facilitate it. They may hoard access, slow down communication, or manipulate what is shared to protect their own status. The same person who connects worlds can also become a bottleneck, limiting collaboration and distorting the original message. This is why transparency and trust are essential qualities in any sustainable network architecture.

Recognizing the power of structural holes also invites the possibility of **network interventions**. These are deliberate actions taken to alter the shape or function of a social network—whether by adding new connections, removing toxic ones, or amplifying underused pathways. For example, in a company where departments operate in silos, introducing cross-functional teams or shared physical spaces can help bridge structural holes. In community organizing, connecting disparate grassroots movements—environmental, economic justice, indigenous rights—can build resilient coalitions that are harder to fragment or co-opt.

These interventions are not limited to physical space. Digital tools can also be deployed to increase or dampen connectivity. Online forums that curate interdisciplinary discussions, mentorship platforms that connect senior professionals with emerging voices from different industries, or databases that map institutional collaborations—all serve to reduce the distance between nodes and increase the fluidity of innovation. But they must be designed thoughtfully. Mere connection is not enough. What matters is **the quality of the exchange**, the trust between actors, and the ability to translate meaning across cultural or epistemological divides.

The deeper insight here is that networks are not just about how many people are connected, but **how they are connected**. Two networks may have the same number of nodes and edges, yet produce vastly different dynamics depending on who serves as the bridges, how inclusive the connections are, and whether the network structure rewards openness or insularity.

The Obscured Principles

Ultimately, the health of any society, organization, or ecosystem depends on its ability to maintain diversity without fragmentation. Micro-communities are essential for belonging and coherence, but without bridges across structural holes, they risk becoming echo chambers. It is through well-designed, well-brokered connections that ideas move from local relevance to systemic transformation. And it is through those same bridges that futures are seeded—not in isolation, but through unexpected collaboration.

5.2 Digital Amplification

If the analog world of influence moves through human relationships and structural bridges, the digital world adds an entirely new layer of complexity—one where scale, speed, and spectacle become defining features. Social media platforms have transformed from mere tools of communication into **global nervous systems**, capable of sensing, reacting, and mobilizing at unprecedented speed. What once took years of organizing or institutional alignment can now unfold in hours. But this amplification comes with costs. The logic of digital networks does not mirror the slow, trust-based rhythms of face-to-face influence. It operates on virality, emotional resonance, and algorithmic selection.

Digital platforms such as Twitter, TikTok, Instagram, and YouTube no longer just reflect public opinion—they **shape it**. Each platform functions as a kind of digital amplifier, elevating certain messages while burying others, often in ways invisible to the users themselves. The key mechanism behind this is the **algorithmic recommendation engine**—a dynamic system that determines what content is surfaced to whom, based on a combination of past behavior, engagement patterns, and predictive modeling.

These algorithms are not neutral. They are designed to maximize engagement, which often means prioritizing content that provokes strong emotional reactions—anger, awe, amusement, fear. As a result, nuance is penalized, subtlety disappears, and the loudest voices rise fastest. In such an environment, attention is no longer a scarce resource—it is a battlefield. The competition is not just for visibility, but for **mental real estate**, for shaping what people see, feel, and act on before conscious reflection even begins.

The Obscured Principles

This has led to a new form of influence strategy: **memetic warfare**. Here, the goal is not to persuade through argument, but to shape perception through symbols, repetition, and emotional contagion. Hashtags become rallying cries. Viral stunts function as cultural signaling. Memes—succinct, emotionally charged, and highly shareable—operate as cognitive Trojan horses, bypassing critical filters and embedding themselves in collective consciousness.

Memetic warfare is not metaphorical. Governments, activist groups, corporations, and ideological movements all now invest heavily in crafting narratives that can gain traction in the memescape. What once required mass media infrastructure can now be launched from a bedroom. A single well-timed meme or hashtag can set the global conversation, dominate news cycles, or destabilize an institution. The boundary between joke and weapon has collapsed.

But this power is not evenly distributed. The design of platforms inherently favors certain actors—those with existing reach, institutional backing, or the resources to game the algorithm. Meanwhile, emerging voices struggle to gain visibility unless they align with the emotional and aesthetic logic of the medium. In this way, amplification does not democratize discourse so much as **restructure its incentives**. The measure of value becomes not truth or coherence, but engagement.

Yet digital amplification also holds radical potential. It has given voice to the previously voiceless, connected distant struggles, and enabled rapid mobilization in the face of injustice. Movements like #BlackLivesMatter, #MeToo, and the global climate strikes began as digital sparks before igniting broader social transformations. In each case, the meme was not just a piece of content—it was a signal, a thread of recognition that connected dispersed individuals into a moment of collective attention.

Still, the speed of digital amplification often outpaces deliberation. Misinformation spreads more quickly than its correction. Outrage cycles burn bright and then vanish, leaving little time for structural change. The internet remembers everything but learns slowly. In this sense, amplification without reflection becomes noise.

To navigate this terrain wisely, we must cultivate new literacies—not just in media consumption, but in narrative design, emotional regulation, and digital ethics. We must understand the dynamics of visibility: how and why something rises, who benefits from that rise, and what gets silenced in the process. Influence in the digital age is no longer about charisma or credentials—it is about mastering the **architecture of amplification**.

Ultimately, the challenge of digital influence is not simply to go viral. It is to go *deep*—to seed ideas that can withstand the churn of the feed, to build networks that can hold complexity, and to create meaning that does not evaporate with the next update. In a world where a single meme can reach millions, the question becomes: What do we want to amplify? And who decides?

Because in the end, the platforms may be artificial, but the consequences are real. The digital web may seem intangible, but it shapes elections, mental health, collective memory, and even the contours of belief itself. The future will not only be built by those who engineer technology, but by those who understand how to guide its amplification toward wisdom, justice, and truth. And that begins with seeing clearly not just what spreads—but *why*.

Chapter 6: Cognitive Architectures — Mind's Blueprint

"We are not thinking machines. We are feeling machines." —

Antonio Damasio

The human mind is not a monolith. It is not a singular entity that perceives, decides, and acts with uniform coherence. Rather, it is a composite architecture—layered, modular, and often contradictory. Beneath the surface of what we call "thought" lie systems with vastly different speeds, goals, and logics. Understanding this internal structure is not a matter of philosophy alone; it is a key to unlocking why we believe what we believe, how we resist change, and what makes us susceptible to manipulation or capable of transformation.

In the modern era, this understanding has deepened through cognitive science and neuroscience, revealing not just that we *can* be irrational, but that we *are*, predictably so, in specific ways. Antonio Damasio's claim that we are feeling machines who think, rather than thinking machines who feel, marks a pivotal reframing of what cognition truly is. Emotions are not interruptions of reason. They are the scaffolding upon which reason is built. Our decisions, our interpretations, even our memories are not purely logical operations but emotionally colored constructions. And at the heart of this lies the interplay between two major modes of cognition: the fast and intuitive, and the slow and deliberate.

6.1 Dual-Process Dynamics

The dual-process model of cognition, made famous by Daniel Kahneman in *Thinking, Fast and Slow*, offers a fundamental framework for understanding how our minds process reality. According to this model, human thinking operates through two distinct but interacting systems. System 1 is fast, automatic, and emotionally driven. It makes snap judgments, leaps to conclusions, and operates with astonishing efficiency. It's what allows you to recognize a friend's face in a crowd, complete the phrase "peanut butter and...," or flinch when a car swerves unexpectedly. It is intuitive and immediate.

System 2, by contrast, is slow, effortful, and analytical. It engages when we solve complex problems, evaluate arguments, or reflect on abstract concepts. It is the system you use when you do mental math, question your own assumptions, or attempt to understand someone else's point of view. But it is also lazy. It requires energy and motivation to engage, and for most of the day, most of us are operating under the governance of System 1.

This division is not merely academic. It explains much of human behavior, from the persistence of cognitive biases to the mechanisms of persuasion, from political polarization to financial irrationality. For example, confirmation bias is primarily a System 1 process—it feels easier to accept information that fits what we already believe. To counteract this, we must engage System 2, which often doesn't happen unless we're explicitly prompted to think critically or emotionally motivated to do so.

Cognitive inertia—our tendency to stick with existing beliefs and frameworks even in the face of new information—is a consequence of this dynamic. It is not that we are incapable of change, but that change is metabolically expensive. Reframing how we see a situation, updating our mental models, or questioning deeply held assumptions all require activation of System 2, and often in direct opposition to System 1's impulses. This inertia is compounded by identity; once a belief is tied to a sense of self or belonging, challenging that belief can feel like an existential threat.

Overcoming cognitive inertia, therefore, is not a purely intellectual process. It demands deliberate strategies that nudge the brain toward openness. One of the most effective approaches is **reframing**—the process of seeing the same situation from a new perspective. Reframing is not simply "thinking differently." It is about interrupting the automatic narrative of System 1 and engaging System 2 long enough to generate alternative interpretations. For example, someone experiencing a professional failure might reflexively interpret it as a sign of personal inadequacy. Reframing that same event as an opportunity for learning or a challenge to resilience requires conscious effort but can radically shift the trajectory of thought and behavior.

Reframing also has collective implications. When societies get stuck in fixed narratives—about security, economics, identity—those narratives become mental defaults, interpreted and reinforced through System 1. Public discourse that enables reframing— through art, storytelling, journalism, or design—can disrupt this inertia and create new cognitive openings. The role of culture, in this sense, becomes the facilitation of reframing on a societal scale.

Yet no amount of reframing is possible without confronting a deeper truth: our cognitive systems are not neutral processors of information. They are emotionally *tagged*. Every perception, memory, or concept is encoded not only with data but with feeling.

This is what Damasio called "somatic markers"—the bodily-based emotional tags that help us prioritize certain options over others. These emotional tags allow us to make decisions quickly and often accurately. But they also lead us astray when feelings override facts, or when emotional tags are manipulated.

Consider how advertising works. Brands do not simply sell products; they attach emotional tags to those products. A luxury car becomes a symbol of status. A sneaker becomes a story of rebellion. A drink becomes an image of belonging. These tags bypass System 2 entirely. They anchor meaning through System 1, which is why people often feel irrationally loyal to a brand or viscerally opposed to another.

The same mechanism is at work in politics. Political figures do not win by delivering the most coherent arguments. They win by attaching emotional tags to concepts. Words like "freedom," "security," "patriotism," or "justice" are not neutral terms. They are emotionally loaded signals, and whoever controls their emotional tag controls the narrative. Once a belief is emotionally encoded— whether through fear, pride, anger, or hope—it becomes difficult to dislodge with facts alone. A policy that activates fear will be opposed instinctively, even if it is logically sound. A slogan that evokes hope will be embraced even if it lacks substance.

This is why emotional intelligence is not merely a soft skill—it is a prerequisite for critical thinking. To think clearly, one must first feel clearly. Recognizing emotional tagging, naming it, and contextualizing it is the beginning of reclaiming agency over our own cognitive architecture. Otherwise, we risk becoming puppets of our own emotional patterns, reacting rather than choosing.

The digital environment further complicates this. Online platforms are designed to engage System 1 relentlessly: headlines crafted to provoke outrage or curiosity, notifications engineered to trigger dopamine, feeds optimized for emotional resonance over informational accuracy. The average person scrolling a social media feed is not deliberating. They are responding—instinctively, emotionally, often unconsciously. In this environment, emotional tags spread faster than reason. A single viral video can shape public perception more powerfully than hours of nuanced analysis.

This is not a call to abandon intuition or suppress emotion. System 1 has immense value. It allows us to navigate daily life efficiently and often wisely. The challenge is not to eliminate System 1 but to know when it is insufficient. It is to recognize the limits of intuition in complex or unfamiliar situations and to cultivate the reflex of *pausing*—of checking in, asking questions, and engaging the slower wisdom of System 2 when necessary.

Education, therefore, should be less about information delivery and more about cognitive design. It should teach people how to know when they are thinking fast versus slow, when they are reacting versus reflecting, and how to create internal architectures that support clarity rather than confusion. This includes mindfulness practices, metacognitive tools, and emotional regulation—skills not traditionally emphasized in formal education, but absolutely essential in an age of cognitive overload.

In the end, our minds are not simply tools for solving problems. They are environments—fluid, adaptive, sometimes chaotic. They are shaped by evolution, by culture, by experience. Understanding their architecture allows us not only to think better, but to live more intentionally. By navigating the interplay between speed and depth, between emotion and logic, between default reactions and chosen responses, we begin to reclaim the most fundamental layer of agency: the architecture of our own perception.

We do not always choose what we feel first. But we can choose how we relate to those feelings. And in that choice lies the doorway from unconscious reflex to conscious meaning. That is the work of cognition—not to remove emotion, but to honor it while building a framework where reason and feeling can collaborate, rather than compete. This is the blueprint of mind—not fixed, but flexing. Not perfect, but improvable. And perhaps, with enough awareness, reprogrammable.

6.2 Identity & Self-Construction

The human mind is not merely a processor of inputs or a logical calculator navigating external stimuli. At its core, it is also a storyteller—an author constantly weaving, editing, and revising a tale called "the self." This tale is not written once and for all; it is dynamic, recursive, and emotionally charged. It functions less as a factual record and more as a **narrative structure**—a psychological architecture that provides continuity, purpose, and direction. We don't just remember our past; we narrate it. And through that narration, we define not only who we were, but who we are and who we might become.

This phenomenon is known as the **narrative self**. Unlike the "experiencing self," which lives moment to moment, the narrative self stitches these moments together into a cohesive story. When we make decisions—particularly ones involving risk, change, or meaning—we consult this internal story more than we realize. The question is not simply "What is the best option?" but rather "What would someone like me do?" or "What fits my story?" This mechanism, while stabilizing, can also become a source of constraint. When the self is overly committed to a certain plotline, growth becomes difficult. People continue in careers, relationships, or ideologies not because they are still fulfilling, but because abandoning them would disrupt the story they've been telling themselves—and others—about who they are.

Every identity is, in a sense, a bundle of internalized stories. These are not created in isolation. From childhood, we absorb scripts from family, culture, media, and social institutions. These scripts include roles: student, achiever, rebel, caretaker, leader, outcast. We internalize expectations about how these roles behave, speak, succeed, fail. This is the territory of **role theory**—the idea that much of human behavior is the performance of culturally defined scripts within specific contexts. We act differently in a job interview than at a dinner with close friends because each context cues a different role, and with it, a different version of the self.

These roles are not inauthentic. They are real and often necessary. They help us navigate complexity, meet social expectations, and coordinate behavior in structured environments. But over time, roles can harden into cages. When the lines between role and self blur, we risk mistaking the part for the whole. A person who identifies entirely as a caregiver may struggle to set boundaries. A lifelong "rationalist" may reject emotional insight even when it's needed. A "rebel" may resist collaboration not out of principle, but out of identity maintenance.

Growth, therefore, often involves a process of **de-anchoring** and **re-anchoring**—letting go of rigid identity constructs and forming new, more flexible ones. De-anchoring does not mean erasing the past. It means loosening its grip. It requires recognizing that the self is a construction, not a given—a dynamic process rather than a fixed essence. This recognition can be destabilizing. It provokes the fear of losing coherence, of not knowing who we are. But it is also the precondition for transformation.

Re-anchoring, by contrast, is the act of building new identity scaffolding. This is done through conscious narrative reframing, through the adoption of new roles, and through the alignment of values and behaviors with emerging aspirations. A person transitioning careers, for example, might initially feel like an imposter. But with time, action, and reflection, they begin to internalize a new story: not one of loss, but of reinvention. What once felt foreign becomes part of the self-narrative. The key is not just external change, but **integration**—bringing the new role into dialogue with the larger story of one's life.

This process is not linear. It involves friction, ambivalence, and regression. But it is also deeply human. We are not fixed identities walking through change. We are changing identities walking through time. The work of self-construction is ongoing. It requires self-awareness, imagination, and courage—not to discover who we are once and for all, but to remain open to who we are still becoming.

This work is all the more critical in a world that rewards fixed identity signals and punishes ambiguity. Social media platforms, institutional labels, and political categories all pressure individuals to simplify themselves for the sake of visibility or belonging. But deep integrity comes not from consistency at all costs, but from the willingness to revise when new insight emerges. The self, at its best, is not a brand. It is a living blueprint—unfinished, iterative, and full of possibility.

6.3 Collective Cognition

While the individual mind is capable of remarkable creativity, insight, and resilience, it is rarely sufficient on its own to navigate the challenges of modern complexity. From scientific discovery to social transformation, from institutional governance to cultural innovation, it is **collective cognition**—the ability of groups to think together—that often determines the shape of the future. Yet group intelligence is not guaranteed. It can produce wisdom or delusion, synthesis or stagnation. The difference lies not in the intelligence of individuals within the group, but in the architecture of their interaction.

The tension between the **wisdom of crowds** and **groupthink** is a case in point. On one hand, when diverse individuals contribute independent judgments to a shared problem—particularly when aggregated effectively—the result can outperform even the best expert. This principle, known as collective intelligence, relies on a few key conditions: diversity of perspective, independence of thought, and effective aggregation mechanisms. When these conditions are met, groups are capable of remarkable feats— predicting election outcomes, solving puzzles, innovating technologies.

On the other hand, when social dynamics dominate—when conformity pressures suppress dissent, when dominant voices monopolize attention, when disagreement is equated with disloyalty—groups can descend into groupthink. In such environments, the appearance of consensus becomes more important than the pursuit of truth. Bad decisions go unchallenged. Warning signs are ignored. Innovation stalls. Groupthink is not simply an error in judgment; it is a failure of process.

This is where **shared mental models** come into play. A shared mental model is a set of implicit understandings that allows group members to anticipate each other's actions, align expectations, and operate with minimal friction. In teams, these models are what allow coordinated performance under pressure. In organizations, they shape culture—how decisions are made, what risks are acceptable, how success is defined. In movements, they form the ideological glue that binds participants together even when strategies diverge.

Shared mental models are powerful, but they are also double-edged. When accurate and flexible, they enable high-functioning groups. When outdated or rigid, they can lead entire institutions astray. A company that views failure as a learning opportunity will innovate differently than one that sees failure as weakness. A movement that embraces complexity will evolve differently than one that demands purity. The health of collective cognition, then, depends on the quality and adaptability of these models.

Designing for effective group intelligence is both art and science. It involves crafting **group processes** that encourage divergence before convergence, that reward contribution over hierarchy, and that build in mechanisms for reflection and revision. Techniques like structured dialogue, rotating facilitation, anonymous input channels, and real-time feedback loops can dramatically enhance a group's capacity for synthesis. So too can rituals that build psychological safety—a sense that disagreement is welcome, that mistakes are part of learning, and that everyone has something to contribute.

Creativity in groups does not emerge from consensus alone. It emerges from **productive tension**—the willingness to hold competing ideas in play long enough for something new to emerge.

This requires time, trust, and often, discomfort. But when the conditions are right, groups can generate insights that no individual alone could have imagined. These are the moments when collaboration becomes not just additive, but transformative.

In larger systems—corporations, cities, nations—the same principles apply. The question is not whether people are smart enough, but whether the system enables their intelligence to surface, connect, and compound. This is the work of **cognitive design** at scale. It involves structuring environments—digital and physical, social and institutional—that invite participation, surface dissent, and reward synthesis. It also means resisting the impulse to centralize cognition in elites. Intelligence is not a rare resource to be concentrated. It is a distributed potential to be activated.

In a time of global interdependence and local fragmentation, designing for collective cognition is not a luxury—it is a necessity. The problems we face—climate disruption, economic inequality, technological ethics—are too complex for top-down solutions or singular visions. They require many minds, many stories, many frames of reference. They require structures that do not merely scale information, but scale *understanding*.

The future belongs to groups that can think together, not because they are uniform, but because they are connected by trust, curiosity, and shared purpose. It belongs to teams that know how to disagree constructively, to communities that can update their models in the face of new evidence, to societies that see diversity not as a liability but as a superpower of cognition.

Collective intelligence is not a given. It must be cultivated, designed, and protected. But when it emerges—when the blueprint of many minds becomes more than the sum of its parts—it offers a glimpse of what humanity, at its best, might yet become.

Chapter 7: Symbolism — The Language of the Hidden

Fact: Symbols process 64× faster in the brain than words.

Human cognition did not evolve with spreadsheets, spreadsheets, or syllogisms. Long before writing systems codified thought and language carried nuance, human beings used marks, images, gestures, and rituals to transmit meaning. A carved animal on a cave wall wasn't just decoration; it was myth, memory, map, and message. Even today, in an era saturated by data and logic, the symbolic remains not only powerful but primary. We decode visual cues faster than we read text. A single image—a flag, a cross, a raised fist—can summon entire worldviews before a sentence even begins.

This chapter explores the architecture of archetypal imagery—those visual forms that carry weight far beyond their apparent simplicity. These symbols function as compressed meaning systems. They bypass rational filters and speak directly to the limbic mind, where instincts, emotions, and values reside. Symbolism is not decoration. It is infrastructure. And for those who understand its grammar, it becomes a powerful tool—sometimes of beauty, sometimes of manipulation, always of influence.

7.1 Archetypal Imagery

Across civilizations and time periods, certain images recur with uncanny frequency. They appear in pottery, banners, currencies, coats of arms, temples, and modern brand logos. These are **power**

symbols—visual motifs that carry associations of sovereignty, dominance, protection, or transcendence. Their persistence suggests something deeper than coincidence. Whether carved in stone or animated on screens, these symbols tap into shared psychological architecture.

Take, for example, the **crown**. Found in the regalia of monarchies from Europe to Asia, it is more than a physical object worn by rulers. It embodies the idea of divine sanction, of elevation above the common. The crown does not only say "this person rules"; it says "this person has been chosen." It transforms authority into sanctity. Its shape—often pointed like rays of light or encircling like a halo—echoes celestial imagery, subtly aligning earthly power with cosmic order.

The **eagle** is another recurring motif. In Roman standards, Nazi iconography, American seals, and countless national emblems, the eagle represents vision, height, and violent force from above. Its ability to soar and strike gives it a dual symbolic role: as guardian and predator. Unlike a dove or a sparrow, the eagle does not beg for peace. It declares watchfulness and the right to intervene. Even when removed from its natural context, it retains a magnetic charge in the human imagination.

Beyond animals and regalia, **totemic forms**—geometric arrangements, hybrid creatures, or ritual objects—often function as visual anchors for a people's story of themselves. These are not just identifiers but repositories of myth. The totem is not powerful because of what it literally depicts, but because of what it evokes: ancestry, protection, taboo, memory. Indigenous cultures preserved entire cosmologies in visual symbols without ever needing alphabetic script. Their meanings were not static; they were lived, updated, and performed across generations.

Modern branding borrows liberally from these ancient playbooks. What used to be carved on stone temples is now burned into consumer consciousness through logos and design systems. This is not cynical imitation—it is strategic engagement with what psychologist Carl Jung called the **collective unconscious**: the reservoir of shared symbolic imagery that continues to shape how humans interpret the world.

The **swoosh of Nike**, the **golden arches of McDonald's**, the **interlocked rings of the Olympics**—these are not just logos. They are **archetypal containers**, designed to invoke feelings and associations before a word is spoken. The Nike swoosh suggests motion, speed, and force. It does not "mean" victory—it *feels* like victory. And because that feeling is consistent, repeated, and emotionally reinforced through advertising and athletic success, it becomes sticky. It implants itself in memory, ready to be triggered at the sight of a shoe, a commercial, a billboard.

This is the essence of **iconic branding**. It does not communicate by explaining, but by patterning. By associating a symbol with a particular emotion or experience, the brand enters the symbolic system of the psyche. It becomes not a product but a character in the consumer's personal mythology. This is why brands often adopt visual language from religion, royalty, or rebellion. They seek not just to sell, but to signify.

But symbolic communication is not limited to the obvious or the iconic. Beneath every visual system—whether it's a fashion aesthetic, a national flag, a political poster, or a music video—lies a field of **visual semiotics**. Semiotics, the study of signs and symbols, helps us understand not just *what* an image is, but *how* it functions. In semiotic terms, a symbol is not just a stand-in for meaning; it is an engine of interpretation. It carries **connotation**—

the emotional, cultural, or ideological context that wraps around its surface.

Consider the simple image of a clenched fist. In one context, it may signify resistance. In another, aggression. Its color, orientation, and accompanying text all shift its interpretation. A black fist raised in protest evokes solidarity and racial justice. A red fist, in a socialist poster, invokes class struggle. The fist itself does not mean one thing; it is a **floating signifier**, acquiring meaning through the system it enters.

The same applies to the **use of color** in visual symbolism. Red may signal danger, urgency, or revolution. Blue may evoke calm, trust, or conservatism. Gold suggests luxury and transcendence. But these associations are not universal; they are culturally constructed and historically contingent. What matters is not just the hue, but the frame. Color becomes a symbolic code, directing attention, evoking emotion, and predisposing belief.

In digital media, these symbolic strategies are often layered. A meme may combine text, image, and gesture to create a new symbolic object—something that feels meaningful even if its literal content is absurd. Political campaigns use visual filters, font choices, and camera angles to signal authority, empathy, or rebellion. The semiotics of a thumbnail can determine whether a video goes viral. These are not random stylistic choices. They are acts of symbolic engineering.

Understanding visual semiotics requires a shift from **seeing to reading**. Not in the sense of decoding a static message, but in sensing the symbolic weight each element carries. Why was that font chosen? Why that crop of the image? Why is the background red, not blue? These questions are not aesthetic—they are interpretive. They reveal the hidden grammar of influence in the visual field.

This is not to say that all symbolism is manipulative. Symbols can also **liberate perception**, awaken memory, or ground abstract truths in accessible forms. Religious iconography, for instance, often serves to anchor transcendence in material forms: the cross, the mandala, the crescent moon. These images are not merely metaphors; they are containers of presence. In contemplative practice, symbolic visualization becomes a doorway to inner states that defy verbal description.

But whether used for commerce, control, or contemplation, symbolism remains a potent force in the architecture of meaning. It accelerates cognition, shapes emotion, and anchors belief. And because it often operates beneath awareness, it is among the most effective—and least examined—tools of persuasion.

To understand the symbolic landscape of a culture is to understand its unconscious. It is to map the images it worships, fears, and internalizes. It is to see not just what people say, but what they *respond to*—instantly, viscerally, without needing explanation.

In this light, symbolic literacy becomes a kind of sovereignty. The ability to read and critique symbols—to see the scaffolding behind the logo, the flag, the slogan—is not just aesthetic awareness. It is psychological defense. It is cultural fluency. It is a way of reclaiming agency in a world where so much of what moves us does so below the threshold of language.

The next time you glance at a screen, a billboard, a product label, or a protest banner, pause. Ask what it is signaling, what it is borrowing, what it is trying to say without saying it. Beneath the surface, the language of the hidden is always speaking. And to those who can hear it, the world becomes not louder, but clearer.

7.2 Ritual & Ceremony

Human beings are not solely rational animals, nor are they purely reactive creatures of instinct. Much of human life unfolds in the symbolic middle ground where meaning is neither thought nor impulse but *performed*. In every culture, across epochs and geographies, ritual and ceremony emerge as tools not merely for communication but for transformation. These are not relics of primitive societies, but sophisticated technologies of meaning. In their repetition, choreography, and dramatic pacing, rituals do not simply reflect the world; they shape it.

Rituals are not limited to religion. They exist in politics, in sports, in family life, in digital spaces. From the handshakes of diplomacy to the singing of national anthems, from courtroom procedures to graduation ceremonies, rituals are carefully constructed sequences of symbolic action designed to mark, move, or sanctify something otherwise intangible. Their power lies in their ability to coordinate bodies and minds around shared intention. When participants step into a ritual space, they are stepping out of ordinary time. They are entering what anthropologist Victor Turner called a *liminal space*—a threshold between what was and what will be.

Liminality is the charged state in which the usual order is suspended and identity becomes fluid. In this suspended state, social norms loosen, hierarchies flatten or invert, and transformation becomes possible. The adolescent on the verge of adulthood, the initiate poised before the secret, the bride and groom in the moment before union—these are all liminal figures. And the ceremonies that surround them are not decorative; they are performative engines that *do* something. They rewire perception, reconfigure relationships, and enact shifts in status that logic alone could never achieve.

Rites of passage are a particularly illuminating example. Whether it's a Bar Mitzvah, a tribal scarification ritual, a military boot camp, or a corporate onboarding retreat, these experiences are more than symbolic markers. They are designed to challenge, disorient, and ultimately recalibrate identity. Often they involve hardship, isolation, or symbolic death. And out of that ordeal, a new social being is born. The group recognizes the transformation not because it has been announced, but because it has been enacted.

This performative power is not inherent to the acts themselves—it is contextual. The meaning of a gesture, a word, or an object depends on where and how it is used. This distinction between the *sacred* and the *profane* is not a quality of the thing itself, but of the setting and the intent. A cup of wine at dinner is one thing; the same wine in a Eucharistic ritual is something else entirely. A circle drawn in the sand during a game of tic-tac-toe has no gravity; the same circle drawn in a ritual context may delineate the boundary between worlds.

By controlling the context, societies control the meaning. Sacred space is often demarcated—architecturally, temporally, socially—to signal a shift in attention and behavior. Shoes are removed, bells are rung, robes are donned. These are not arbitrary acts. They are sensory cues that mark the passage from the ordinary to the extraordinary. They prepare the body and the mind to enter a different mode of engagement. And once inside, the rules of causality may no longer apply. Mythic time unfolds. The dead are remembered. The future is invoked. The invisible becomes palpable.

This is why authoritarian regimes often attempt to co-opt ritual: to dress their power in the trappings of sacred performance. Parades, slogans, uniforms, chants—all borrow from the logic of ceremony. They manufacture gravity. They mimic the drama of collective transformation, even when the underlying reality remains oppressive or stagnant. Likewise, commercial culture imitates ritual through product launches, brand activations, and choreographed advertising campaigns. The aim is the same: to embed the product, ideology, or identity in the deeper channels of emotional and symbolic resonance.

But rituals can also be sites of resistance. Subversive ceremonies, counter-cultural performances, and unsanctioned rites can reclaim meaning from dominant systems. Flash mobs, protest marches, street theatre—these are modern rituals that operate in public space, reactivating the performative power of collective presence. Even in the digital realm, rituals adapt: live-streamed ceremonies, hashtag campaigns, and coordinated digital silence all function as choreographed acts of meaning-making.

What becomes clear is that ritual is not obsolete. It is perennial. It evolves with context but retains its structural function: to mark transitions, to bind groups, and to embody values. And because it operates below the threshold of explicit argument, it can accomplish what information cannot. It can persuade without persuading. It can move people who cannot be convinced.

To live without ritual is not to live rationally—it is to drift without anchor. Without ceremonies to punctuate time and mark meaning, life becomes a blur of events without interpretation. In this way, ritual is not mere ornament. It is the grammar of belonging, the architecture of significance. And to reimagine our rituals is to reimagine who we are—together.

7.3 Code Systems

While rituals embody meaning in movement and gesture, **code systems** embed it in structure—numbers, calendars, symbols, and scripts that organize perception across time and space. These systems are not always overt. They may operate beneath the surface, in secret or encrypted forms, shaping behavior, belief, and belonging through abstraction. But whether revealed or hidden, these codes function as vessels of power. They encode not only information but worldview.

Among the oldest and most enduring of these systems is **numerology**—the attribution of symbolic or mystical significance to numbers. In ancient traditions from Pythagorean Greece to Hebrew Kabbalah to Chinese cosmology, numbers were not mere quantities. They were qualities, each bearing unique spiritual weight. The number seven, for instance, recurs in religious and natural systems: seven days of creation, seven chakras, seven heavens. Twelve marks the passage of time in zodiac signs and months. Three implies harmony or resolution. These numbers were not chosen randomly; they formed a language of resonance, a map of cosmic structure.

Closely linked to numerology are **mythic calendars**—systems of time that do not merely measure duration but assign meaning to its passage. The Mayan Long Count, the Vedic Yugas, the Islamic Hijri calendar, the Gregorian liturgical year—all organize human life within a symbolic framework. Days become sacred. Years carry prophecies. Eclipses, solstices, and planetary alignments are not meteorological events but messages. These calendars do not only tell us what time it is; they tell us what *kind* of time it is—what is permitted, expected, feared, or celebrated.

In parallel, **secret scripts** and encoded languages have functioned as both barriers and gateways. Esoteric traditions often rely on specialized writing systems—runes, glyphs, ciphers—not only to obscure their teachings but to frame them as sacred. To decode the symbol is to undergo an initiation. Mystery schools across time have used layered symbols to separate the uninitiated from the elect. The Rosicrucians, the Freemasons, the Hermeticists—all wove symbolic geometries and textual veils around their cosmologies. In these contexts, secrecy is not a failure of openness but a methodology of reverence. Knowledge is earned, not consumed.

These esoteric systems did not vanish with the rise of modernity. They morphed. Today, **modern cults** and ideological echo chambers often mimic the structure of mystery traditions. They develop insider terminology, symbolic hierarchies, and cryptic initiation rituals. Some do this intentionally, others through cultural evolution. In both cases, the effect is the same: to create a sense of exclusivity, to bond members through shared secrets, and to exert control over meaning.

In the digital age, the metaphor of secrecy becomes literal. **Encryption**—the process of converting information into code to prevent unauthorized access—now serves as the backbone of communication and commerce. But encryption also functions symbolically. It has become a metaphor for mistrust, for complexity, for hidden truth. The rise of decentralized technologies, anonymous browsing, and cryptographic currencies has reframed power around the ability to *encode* and *decode*. Who has the keys? Who understands the algorithm? Who controls access?

This shift transforms our cultural imagination. Encryption is no longer merely technical. It becomes **metaphysical**. The encrypted file, the hidden server, the blockchain ledger—all become symbols of a world in which reality is layered, concealed, and conditionally accessible. Even conspiracy theories adopt cryptographic language. "Do your own research" becomes a call to decipher hidden codes. "The elites" become a shadowy priesthood with exclusive access to symbolic truth.

In this landscape, **code literacy** becomes power. To understand symbolic systems, whether ancient or algorithmic, is to navigate a deeper layer of meaning. It is to see patterns where others see noise. It is to recognize that beneath the surface of events lie scripts—sometimes literal, often metaphorical—that organize perception and guide behavior.

But there is a danger here. Symbolic literacy can devolve into symbolic fetishism. The desire for hidden meaning can lead to paranoia, esotericism for its own sake, or ideological rigidity. Codes can liberate or imprison. They can awaken or delude. The key distinction is whether the system is **generative or closed**. Does it invite interpretation, or does it shut it down? Does it deepen awareness, or merely reinforce identity?

Ultimately, the symbolic codes that structure human reality are not static. They evolve with consciousness. From ancient glyphs to modern algorithms, from ritual numerologies to digital encryption, we see a continuity of purpose: to give shape to the unseen, to control the boundaries of knowledge, and to organize the mystery of existence into legible forms.

To read the world as code is not to become paranoid. It is to become attuned. It is to realize that symbols are not mere signs—they are architectures of power, gateways of transformation, and mirrors of the psyche. And in a world increasingly shaped by abstraction, learning to read those mirrors may be the most important kind of literacy we can cultivate.

Chapter 8: Economic Backbones —
Underlying Currents

Statistic: 1% of transactions generate 50% of systemic volatility.

To understand the world through the lens of power, reality, and destiny, one must eventually peer beneath the surface of visible economic activity. Here, beneath the polished façade of formal markets and sanctioned institutions, lies a far less visible—but vastly more influential—substratum: the realm of hidden markets. These markets, though not always illegal, often operate outside the scope of mainstream regulation and public understanding. They do not appear on televised financial reports or public GDP statements. Yet, in many ways, they dictate the rhythm and vulnerability of the global economy.

The term "economic backbone" typically evokes industrial infrastructure, trade flows, and employment numbers. But such a view only scratches the surface. Beneath these observable currents exist subterranean forces—dense, obscure, and often intentionally opaque. These forces shape the very conditions under which official economies function, expand, and collapse. If we think of economies as iceberg systems, the publicly visible segment represents only a fraction of their true dynamics. Hidden markets, then, form the submerged mass—immense in influence, precarious in design.

Among the most significant players in this underworld of finance is the system known as **shadow banking**. Though it sounds conspiratorial, shadow banking refers to a vast network of financial intermediaries that function much like banks—but without the same oversight. Hedge funds, structured investment vehicles

(SIVs), money market funds, and repurchase agreements (repos) all play roles in this space. What unites them is not illegality, but informality. These entities move capital, extend credit, and facilitate liquidity without falling under the traditional purview of central banks or regulatory institutions.

At the height of the 2008 global financial crisis, the systemic importance—and danger—of shadow banking became terrifyingly apparent. Subprime mortgage packages were bundled into collateralized debt obligations, sliced, repackaged, and sold across continents. Many of these products existed off the balance sheets of the banks that birthed them. These **off-balance-sheet vehicles**, while nominally separate, were often tied to parent institutions in ways that magnified risk. When one node in this fragile web failed, the ripple effects cascaded globally.

Such instruments allowed risk to be hidden in plain sight, obscured behind acronyms, exotic financial engineering, and a labyrinth of counterparty relationships. Regulators found themselves unable to map the contagion, not due to malice, but due to the **opacity** of the system. What this exposed was not just financial instability, but a profound philosophical truth: that visibility is not the same as reality. What is unrecorded is not necessarily unimportant. In fact, in modern finance, the opposite often holds true.

Yet not all hidden markets function at the scale or with the abstraction of shadow banking. There are also **parallel economies**—localized systems of exchange that exist alongside formal structures, often in response to their failures. These include barter systems, time banks, informal lending circles, and, more recently, cryptocurrency enclaves. Such systems emerge out of necessity, especially in environments where trust in official currencies or institutions has eroded.

Take, for example, the rise of **barter networks** in countries experiencing hyperinflation. When paper money becomes worthless, people revert to the oldest economic principle: direct exchange. Goods and services are traded without the mediation of currency, creating a value system based not on fiat, but on perceived utility. In such systems, value becomes hyper-localized and often more **resilient** than the collapsing national economy.

Cryptocurrencies represent a different kind of parallel economy—one rooted not in locality but in **decentralized technology**. Bitcoin, Ethereum, and other blockchain-based assets were conceived not merely as alternative currencies but as ideological projects: tools to bypass centralized control, enable peer-to-peer exchange, and resist surveillance. Within their code is a vision of sovereignty, privacy, and transparency—although ironically, these networks often require **technical literacy** and **infrastructural privilege** to access.

Within these crypto enclaves, entire economic subcultures have emerged. Some mirror traditional financial instruments—exchanges, derivatives, lending protocols—while others innovate entirely new models such as decentralized autonomous organizations (DAOs) and non-fungible tokens (NFTs). The speed and anonymity of these systems allow for rapid experimentation. But they also create a haven for **regulatory arbitrage**, where participants seek jurisdictions or platforms that offer minimal oversight, opening the door to scams, pump-and-dump schemes, and manipulation at scale.

Beyond the philosophical or technological dimensions of these alternative economies lies another domain entirely: the **dark web**. Often caricatured in media, the dark web is not inherently criminal. It is a segment of the internet accessible only through specialized tools like Tor browsers, where anonymity is the default setting. Within its encrypted corridors, however, flourish some of the most unregulated and ethically ambiguous forms of trade.

From illicit drugs and counterfeit documents to hacking services and human trafficking networks, the dark web hosts a shadow economy that eludes taxation, regulation, and often detection. Its most famous platform, Silk Road, operated as an underground marketplace that accepted only cryptocurrencies and used sophisticated reputation systems to maintain trust. Its shutdown in 2013 did not extinguish such markets. Others quickly rose to take its place, adapting, fragmenting, and becoming harder to trace.

What makes these markets particularly resilient is not only their technological infrastructure but their **socioeconomic logic**. They respond to demand that exists independently of law: the demand for privacy, access, speed, and control. And while law enforcement agencies have improved their capacity to track blockchain transactions and infiltrate marketplaces, the arms race between regulation and circumvention remains ongoing.

Importantly, the impact of hidden markets is not limited to the transactions that take place within them. Their existence **shapes the incentives and behaviors** of formal markets as well. When hedge funds factor in potential crypto arbitrage, when banks worry about capital flight into decentralized platforms, when regulators attempt to balance innovation with security, they are all responding to the gravitational pull of hidden systems. These forces may be unseen, but they are anything but negligible.

Moreover, the psychological dimension cannot be ignored. Hidden markets invoke not just profit motives, but narratives of freedom, secrecy, rebellion, and escape. They are arenas of myth as much as of math. For many participants, especially in marginalized or surveilled populations, these markets represent autonomy in a system that otherwise excludes or exploits them. This emotional and symbolic charge is as important as any financial analysis.

To study hidden markets, then, is not just to analyze risk or detect fraud. It is to recognize the **multi-layered nature of economic reality**. It is to see that formal markets are only one interface— perhaps the most visible, but not the most fundamental. Beneath them lie structures that are more fluid, more volatile, and often more powerful in shaping collective outcomes.

This realization invites both caution and creativity. Caution, because ignoring these systems can blindside policy and destabilize institutions. Creativity, because engaging with them offers insight into how economies adapt, mutate, and evolve in response to stress, constraint, and desire.

The backbone of an economy is not a singular thing. It is a latticework—of systems seen and unseen, sanctioned and unsanctioned, centralized and decentralized. Understanding it requires more than data. It requires perception attuned to the subterranean, imagination that can model the unofficial, and courage to look where most prefer not to.

In the next section, we will explore the leverage points—legal, psychological, technological—that allow these hidden systems to influence global stability and volatility. For now, it is enough to say: what is hidden is not irrelevant. It is, in many cases, the engine of the visible. And only by tracing its contours can we begin to map the true architecture of economic power.

8.1 Value Extraction

At the heart of every economic system lies a tension between what is *produced* and what is *captured*. Not all wealth is created by adding value. Much of it—arguably the majority in late-stage capitalist structures—is extracted through mechanisms that allow entities to intercept flows of value rather than generate them. This distinction is foundational. It separates innovation from exploitation, creation from capture, and builders from gatekeepers.

Value extraction often masquerades as productivity. Yet it operates through structural positions of advantage, not through innovation or improvement. This is best understood through the concept of **rent-seeking**—an economic term that describes the act of increasing one's share of existing wealth without creating new wealth. Classic rent-seeking behavior includes monopolistic practices, regulatory manipulation, and intellectual enclosures. Unlike entrepreneurs who take risks to deliver new products or services, rent-seekers leverage control—over land, licenses, or intellectual property—to skim off the top of productive activity.

Consider the realm of **intellectual property**. What was once designed to incentivize creativity and safeguard authorship has, in many contexts, become a labyrinth of tollbooths. These tollbooths are not visible on highways, but embedded in code, patents, licenses, and digital rights management. Corporations and holding firms often accumulate intellectual property not to innovate, but to litigate. They build portfolios of patents not for development, but for deterrence—weaponizing ownership as leverage.

This enclosure of knowledge can be seen in pharmaceutical patents that keep life-saving drugs priced out of reach, in academic publishing monopolies that profit from publicly funded research, and in software ecosystems where interoperability is restricted to preserve market dominance. What is being monetized is not always the invention itself, but the **right to exclude** others from using or adapting it. The toll is invisible, but pervasive.

Even more insidious is the architecture of **platform capitalism**— the dominant model of digital economy today. Here, the product is not a good or service, but the user. Platforms like social networks, search engines, and e-commerce giants do not primarily create content; they aggregate, curate, and monetize the behaviors of their users. Every scroll, click, and pause becomes data. That data becomes a behavioral profile. And those profiles are auctioned in real-time to advertisers, political operatives, and algorithmic models.

The genius—and danger—of platform capitalism lies in its recursive loop: the more attention it captures, the more data it extracts; the more data it extracts, the better it becomes at capturing attention. This is not rent in the traditional sense. It is the construction of behavioral highways where the toll is not paid in money, but in *time, focus*, and *cognitive sovereignty*.

In this model, value is extracted not through sale but through surveillance. The user becomes the worker, the product, and the customer simultaneously. The labor of interaction—commenting, uploading, reacting—is unpaid. The platform's revenue, however, is massive. And its control over economic flows extends not only through profit, but through **infrastructure**. Entire industries— from journalism to entertainment, from small business marketing to education—now depend on platforms for distribution and visibility.

This extraction model also displaces traditional forms of competition. In the industrial age, competition happened at the level of product or price. In the platform age, competition is often eliminated through **network effects**. The more users a platform has, the more valuable it becomes—not just to users, but to everyone who depends on access to them. This self-reinforcing advantage allows platforms to operate as de facto monopolies while maintaining the illusion of user choice.

Yet perhaps the most profound cost of value extraction in platform economies is not financial, but **epistemological**. These systems increasingly mediate what people see, believe, and desire. They do not simply extract attention; they *shape it*. They curate reality. They determine which voices rise and which vanish. And in doing so, they become gatekeepers of the symbolic economy—the economy of meaning, trust, and perceived truth.

To understand value extraction, then, is not only to critique unfair profit mechanisms. It is to diagnose how modern economies prioritize capture over contribution, enclosure over expansion, and influence over substance. It is to ask not only *who profits*, but *who decides* what value is, where it lives, and how it moves.

8.2 Resource Scarcity & Allocation

While digital economies have abstracted much of modern value into data, reputation, and symbols, the real world still runs on matter: electricity, water, minerals, and physical networks. And in that material substrate lies another layer of hidden power. The control of **scarce resources**—not just their ownership, but their allocation—defines the boundary between abundance and precarity, between dominance and dependence.

The fiction of infinite growth collides with the reality of finite supply. The world's most critical materials are not evenly distributed. Some lie in politically unstable regions; others are hidden beneath sovereign borders or contested terrain. Among these, **energy** remains the most volatile. Oil and gas continue to serve as geopolitical levers, their supply chains embedded in treaties, pipelines, and military alliances. The control of fossil fuels is not merely an economic issue—it is an instrument of coercion, often deciding the outcome of conflicts and the viability of states.

Even as renewable energy rises, the dependencies shift rather than disappear. The production of solar panels, wind turbines, and electric batteries requires **rare earth elements**—a category of seventeen metals with names like neodymium and dysprosium, which are critical for magnets, displays, and green technologies. China currently dominates the mining and processing of these elements, creating a new form of **strategic asymmetry**. Access to the future now requires dependence on a highly centralized present.

Water, though often ignored in macroeconomic discourse, may be the defining resource of the coming century. As aquifers are depleted, rivers redirected, and rainfall patterns disrupted, water security becomes a source of tension between regions and nations. The privatization of water infrastructure, especially in developing countries, transforms access into a commodity. In megacities and drought-prone regions, water has become more expensive than fuel. Yet its infrastructure remains vulnerable: dams, pumps, and pipelines can be sabotaged, weaponized, or simply allowed to decay.

Layered on top of these material resources are **geo-economic chokepoints**—narrow corridors through which vast quantities of goods, data, or energy must pass. The Strait of Hormuz, the Panama Canal, the Suez Canal, the Strait of Malacca—these are not merely maritime passages. They are levers of global stability. When a single ship blocks the Suez Canal, trillions in commerce are disrupted. When tensions rise near the Strait of Hormuz, oil prices spike worldwide. These chokepoints are **infrastructural pressure points**, where sabotage, blockade, or political instability can ripple across the planet in hours.

In the digital realm, **undersea data cables** function as equally critical arteries. Over 95% of global internet traffic passes through them, yet they are fragile and largely unprotected. A single severed cable can isolate nations or cripple sectors. The entities that control or monitor these cables—corporate or national—wield disproportionate power over the flow of information, surveillance capacity, and even financial transactions.

In parallel, another layer of power operates through **futures markets**. These are not markets for current supply, but for *expectations* of future scarcity or abundance. Investors and speculators place bets on tomorrow's deficits—of wheat, oil, lithium, even water. These markets were originally designed for stability, allowing producers to hedge against price fluctuations. But in recent decades, they have become speculative arenas where large

110

institutional players can manipulate perceptions of scarcity for profit.

The psychological dimension of these markets is profound. Anticipation itself becomes value. If enough traders believe that a drought will impact grain prices, their collective behavior can drive prices up *before* the drought even occurs. In this way, futures markets are not reflections of reality—they are engines of it. They shape farmer decisions, national reserves, and even geopolitical strategy.

Scarcity, therefore, is not always natural. It is often **manufactured or exaggerated** through perception, control, and speculative dynamics. Allocation becomes a function of **power**, not just supply. Who gets what, when, and how is not dictated by fairness or need, but by leverage, foresight, and access to information.

This raises critical ethical and strategic questions. Should water be tradable on futures exchanges? Should data cables be militarized? Should rare earth elements be governed by cartel-like structures? These are not hypothetical concerns. They are unfolding dilemmas at the intersection of economics, security, and survival.

To track resource scarcity is to track the slow-motion redrawing of global power maps. And to understand allocation is to understand the choreography behind the curtain—how decisions made in boardrooms, ministries, or trading floors determine whether a village gets electricity, whether a region survives a heatwave, or whether a nation retains its independence.

In the end, the economy is not a machine but a system of prioritization. It tells us what we value by how we allocate what is limited. And those allocations are never neutral. They are encoded with ideology, strategy, and often inequality.

Hidden markets may operate in shadows. Value extraction may hide behind innovation. But when it comes to scarcity and allocation, the stakes become starkly material. Here, power is not abstract. It is measurable—in megawatts, in barrels, in liters, in lives.

Chapter 9: Technological Algorithms — Digital Power Grids

"Algorithms are opinions embedded in code." — Cathy O'Neil

We often speak of laws as things made in parliaments, enforced by police, interpreted by judges. But in the 21st century, the most consequential laws are not passed by legislative bodies. They are written in programming languages. They do not come with ceremony or debate. They emerge silently, deployed in the background of everyday life, governing what we see, what we're allowed to do, what we're told, and what we believe. This is the reality of algorithmic governance—a silent, ever-expanding infrastructure that now shapes the architecture of our choices.

At its most basic, an algorithm is a set of instructions. But modern algorithms are not linear recipes—they are complex, self-adapting systems, trained on oceans of data, built to anticipate, nudge, rank, categorize, and judge. They perform functions that were once the sole domain of human intuition or institutional protocol. They assign creditworthiness, predict criminal behavior, determine medical eligibility, recommend parole decisions, filter job applicants, and decide which content we consume online. And yet, despite this growing role, algorithms operate largely in **black boxes**—hidden from scrutiny, shielded by proprietary rights, and often too complex even for their creators to fully understand.

In this context, "code as law" is not a metaphor—it is a structural shift. Algorithms now act as regulators of behavior, enforcers of norms, and arbiters of opportunity. Their judgments are often more decisive than human ones, precisely because they are automated.

There is no delay, no fatigue, no ambiguity. But therein lies the danger. Automation can amplify injustice when it codifies bias as logic. And it often does so under the guise of neutrality.

Take, for instance, credit scoring systems. These tools determine not only whether someone can buy a house or car, but often whether they can rent an apartment, get a job, or access healthcare. The data points used may include income, debt levels, and payment history—but also zip codes, shopping habits, and even social connections. When a person is reduced to a score, nuance is lost. And when that score is generated by an opaque algorithm, recourse becomes nearly impossible.

Similarly, predictive policing algorithms analyze historical crime data to forecast where crime is most likely to occur. But what if that data is skewed by decades of over-policing in minority neighborhoods? The algorithm learns from the past—and repeats it. It sends more officers to already surveilled areas, finds more crime because it is looking for it there, and reinforces the data it was trained on. A feedback loop of bias disguised as objectivity.

This same logic infects the criminal justice system. Risk assessment tools are now used in sentencing decisions, assigning scores to defendants based on their likelihood of reoffending. These scores may be derived from factors like employment status, neighborhood, family background, or prior arrests. But none of this is immutable truth—it is socially conditioned data. The algorithm may claim to predict behavior, but in reality, it mirrors inequality. A low-income individual with a petty record may be rated riskier than a high-income individual with a violent offense, simply because the inputs are stacked against the former.

And then there is the world of **content moderation**—where algorithms decide which voices are amplified, which are silenced, and which simply never appear. These systems sort billions of posts every day across social media platforms. They flag misinformation, hate speech, graphic content—but also satire, dissent, or non-Western cultural expressions, depending on how the model was trained. Errors in moderation don't just inconvenience people. They erase speech, dismantle communities, and skew public discourse. Worse, users often have no idea why a post was removed or an account shadowbanned. The system decides, but rarely explains.

This lack of **transparency** is no accident. Most algorithms used in governance, commerce, and media are considered intellectual property. Companies argue that their models are trade secrets, and regulators often lack the technical expertise or legal authority to demand access. Even when source code is shared, it may be incomprehensible—millions of lines of logic trained on proprietary data, influenced by constantly shifting variables. The algorithm is not a single object. It is a living, evolving entity that defies fixed accountability.

This has led to growing calls for **algorithmic auditing**—a field dedicated to uncovering how automated systems work, where their biases lie, and what their real-world impacts are. Auditing an AI model is not like auditing a financial statement. It requires reverse engineering decisions, stress-testing predictions, analyzing datasets, and mapping correlations that may be statistically accurate but ethically fraught. Researchers have found that facial recognition tools are less accurate for darker skin tones, that hiring algorithms can penalize applicants based on gendered patterns in resumes, and that recommendation engines often drive users toward extremism to maximize engagement.

The problem is not that these systems make mistakes. The problem is that they **scale those mistakes** across entire populations, institutionalizing them in ways that are difficult to challenge. A biased judge can be removed. A flawed law can be repealed. But an algorithm deployed across jurisdictions, industries, and languages becomes invisible infrastructure. It ceases to be seen as a decision-maker and instead becomes a condition of reality. The map becomes the territory.

Compounding this is the psychological effect of interacting with automated authority. People are more likely to accept an algorithmic decision without question—especially when it is presented as scientific or data-driven. This creates a chilling atmosphere in which users internalize the logic of the machine, adjusting their behavior to avoid punishment or exclusion. We optimize ourselves for visibility, for engagement, for the metrics that algorithms reward. And in doing so, we risk becoming flattened versions of ourselves—predictable, modelable, marketable.

Yet the alternative is not to abandon algorithms. It is to **reclaim them**—to build systems that are transparent, accountable, and participatory. Open-source models, democratic oversight, algorithmic impact assessments, and ethical AI frameworks are emerging as countermeasures. But they require more than good intentions. They require infrastructure. Institutions. Legal scaffolding that treats code not as magic, but as policy.

Because when code becomes law, those who write it wield disproportionate power. And when that code is unaccountable, the society it governs becomes brittle. The promise of automation was to liberate us from bias, inefficiency, and error. But without vigilance, it merely launders those flaws through silicon logic. The question is no longer whether we will be governed by algorithms. The question is **whose values they encode**—and whether we are allowed to see what those values are.

In a digital world, sovereignty is increasingly exercised through code. And if we are to retain agency within that world, we must learn to read the algorithms as we once read constitutions. Not just for their syntax, but for their assumptions. Not just for what they do, but for what they *believe*.

9.1 Network Effects & Lock-in

To grasp how power operates in the digital age, one must understand a deceptively simple idea: the more people use a system, the harder it becomes to leave. This is the heart of what economists call **network effects**—the principle that a service becomes more valuable the more people join it. But what begins as a user-friendly convenience quickly becomes a mechanism of dominance. The Facebook of today is not the garage project it once was; it is an empire of entanglement, in which billions of users are simultaneously customers, content creators, and captive audiences.

Network effects are not inherently sinister. Language, currency, and road systems are all historical examples—shared protocols that facilitate coordination. But when they manifest in closed, profit-driven systems, they create what is called **lock-in**. Lock-in occurs when switching to an alternative is so costly—in terms of data, relationships, habits, or access—that people remain within a system not out of preference, but necessity. In such systems, the company doesn't have to be the best, just entrenched enough to be unavoidable.

Consider the dominance of operating systems or productivity software. For many individuals and organizations, using alternatives isn't just inconvenient—it can be economically or socially damaging. Entire workflows are structured around proprietary tools. Compatibility becomes currency. A document written in one platform may lose fidelity in another. Teams trained on one interface may need weeks to adapt to a new one. The friction isn't technological—it's behavioral, cultural, and structural.

This dynamic is magnified in **platform monopolies**. Amazon, Apple, Google, and Meta are no longer simply companies; they are **infrastructures**. They set the terms of access, shape market dynamics, and often serve as both player and referee in the ecosystems they govern. A company that wants to reach customers online may have no choice but to advertise on Google, list on Amazon, or engage on Instagram. These are not just platforms. They are digital nation-states, with borders defined by code, citizenship granted through terms of service, and disputes resolved internally—often without appeal.

Lock-in is reinforced by **technical standards** that function as de-facto regulations. When one format becomes ubiquitous—whether a video codec, a payment system, or a messaging protocol—it effectively dictates the rules for participation. Companies that control those standards wield enormous influence. They decide who can plug in, under what terms, and at what cost. Sometimes, these standards are openly negotiated and globally agreed upon. But more often, they emerge through dominance, not consensus.

The challenge is that breaking free from lock-in is not just a technical feat—it is a political one. **Open protocols**—shared, non-proprietary formats that allow interoperability—are one answer. They allow innovation without central permission, enabling new actors to enter the ecosystem without starting from scratch. The early internet was built on such protocols: email, HTTP, DNS. These were the foundational rails upon which creativity could flourish. But as commercialization accelerated, proprietary systems replaced open ones. Walls went up. Gardens were walled.

Now, a new generation of decentralization technologies—most notably blockchain and peer-to-peer networks—seeks to reverse this enclosure. These systems are not simply alternatives; they are attempts to rethink the architecture of digital power. A decentralized identity, for example, allows a person to carry their data, credentials, and social graph across platforms. A decentralized web allows publishing without centralized hosting. These are early, imperfect experiments—but they reveal a deeper truth: the internet does not have to be the way it is. Its centralization is a choice, not a law of nature.

Still, the path out of lock-in is steep. Incumbents have vast resources to absorb or neutralize threats. They buy competitors before they grow, change APIs to block interoperability, or flood emerging spaces with alternatives that dilute their promise. And users, conditioned by habit, often find comfort in the familiar— even when it constrains them.

In the end, the struggle against lock-in is a struggle for **agency**. It is about whether we use tools, or tools use us. Whether we can exit systems without losing our identities, our histories, or our voices. It is about the ability to migrate—not just physically, but digitally. And in a world where code defines reality, that ability may be the new face of freedom.

9.2 Cyber-Psychological Operations

If the twentieth century was defined by propaganda as a blunt instrument—posters, speeches, and broadcasts aimed at shaping mass opinion—then the twenty-first is characterized by **precision-guided persuasion**. Not slogans, but signals. Not leaflets, but likes. The battlefield is no longer a field. It is a feed. And the weapons are not bombs or bullets, but algorithms, metrics, and psychological levers.

Welcome to the age of **cyber-psychological operations**, where the manipulation of belief, emotion, and behavior happens not through coercion, but through calibration. Where influence is not broadcast to the many, but tailored to the one. This is not dystopian fiction. It is how digital advertising already works.

At the core of this architecture is the practice of **nudging**—a concept from behavioral economics that involves steering people toward certain choices without eliminating alternatives. In the online context, nudging occurs through interface design, notification timing, choice architecture, and algorithmic curation. Every time you are offered a "default" setting, a limited range of options, or a frictionless path toward purchase, your autonomy is being shaped. You are not being forced. You are being **guided**— with data, with design, and with deep knowledge of your habits.

Platforms conduct **A/B testing** on millions of users simultaneously, tweaking everything from button color to headline phrasing. These micro-experiments are not trivial. They determine what makes you stay, click, buy, share, or believe. In this framework, the user becomes both the subject and the specimen. The digital environment is not passive. It is *engineered for effect.*

But nudging is only one layer. A darker stratum lies beneath: the fabrication of reality itself. **Deepfakes**, synthetic voices, and AI-generated personas are making it increasingly difficult to distinguish truth from fabrication. A fake video of a politician can be generated, shared, and believed before fact-checkers even mobilize. A synthetic influencer—composed entirely of code—can attract sponsorships, followers, and fan devotion without ever having drawn breath.

These tools do not merely distort reality. They **fracture trust**. In an environment where anything can be faked, people begin to doubt everything. And in that doubt, manipulators thrive. Propaganda no longer needs to convince people of one lie. It merely needs to **exhaust** them with noise, until they lose faith in their own perception. This is epistemic erosion. And it is as dangerous as any cyberattack on infrastructure.

In response, some states and organizations are beginning to build **defensive architectures**. These include authenticity verification tools, content provenance frameworks, and resilient communication protocols. The goal is not to eliminate manipulation entirely—that is impossible—but to make systems more **robust**, transparent, and accountable. Just as societies developed public health systems to respond to biological threats, we now require **cognitive health systems**—institutions and technologies designed to protect the integrity of information ecosystems.

This means rethinking not just regulation, but design. It means creating platforms where dissent can flourish without being hijacked by bots. It means equipping individuals with media literacy, not as a school subject, but as a survival skill. It means questioning the incentives of systems that reward outrage, polarization, and performative extremism. Because if the algorithm thrives on division, then unity becomes an act of resistance.

But above all, it means recognizing that cyber-psychological operations are not a side effect. They are the new frontier. Influence has gone granular. Persuasion has gone ambient. And unless we learn to see the strings—who is pulling them, why, and how—we will continue to dance in a theater not of our choosing.

The goal, then, is not to retreat from the digital world, but to reclaim it. To build systems that reflect our values, not just our vulnerabilities. To demand transparency, without sacrificing innovation. And to remember that in the end, the most powerful defense against manipulation is not a stronger filter, but a deeper *awareness*.

Because in a world where the battlefield is perception, clarity becomes the most radical form of resistance.

Chapter 10: Synthesis — Mastering the Obscured Principles

"To know your enemy, you must become your enemy." — *Sun Tzu*

The world is not flat. It is layered. And within those layers lie systems—nested, intersecting, and often concealed—shaping everything from the stock market to social movements, from our personal identities to geopolitical trajectories. By now, we've pulled back many veils: examining power as it operates beyond institutions, reality as it is constructed rather than perceived, and destiny as a product of emergent forces and encoded expectations. But knowledge alone is not mastery. To engage with the obscured principles is to go further—to begin mapping them, aligning them, and using them as instruments of both insight and action.

This final phase is not a conclusion. It is a convergence. To master the obscured is to move from passive understanding to active configuration. It is the recognition that these systems do not simply exist; they are maintained and manipulated by people, ideologies, and mechanisms. If we are not shaping them, we are being shaped by them.

The first step toward mastery is **integration**—the ability to map interdependencies among power, perception, and projection. Each dimension influences the others in feedback loops that are often invisible but deeply consequential. A belief (symbolic reality) shapes how a group organizes (social power), which in turn influences how events unfold (emergent destiny). A platform's algorithm (informational architecture) elevates specific content, which reshapes political discourse (collective cognition), which drives changes in law and policy (formal structures of power).

These links do not run in one direction. They spiral, loop, and compound. Consider a single event—an economic shock, a viral video, a scientific breakthrough. What begins in one layer quickly cascades through others. A financial collapse (physical/economic) erodes institutional trust (symbolic), which triggers mass protests (social), which are amplified through meme ecologies (informational), which provoke state responses (power), which reshape norms and expectations (destiny). If we analyze these layers in isolation, we miss the choreography. Mastery requires not compartmentalization, but pattern recognition across the full system.

One useful metaphor is that of a **multi-tiered operating system**. At the hardware level lies the material infrastructure: energy grids, supply chains, servers, borders. On top of that runs software—our information flows, platforms, currencies, bureaucracies. But what guides the behavior of the software is something subtler: the *firmware* of society—the underlying myths, identities, symbols, and unspoken rules. A master of the obscured does not just hack one level. They understand how a change in one tier reconfigures the others.

This is the principle of **cross-layer strategy**—a technique that aligns interventions across different levels of influence to create durable transformation. A political movement that only protests on the street (physical) may gain visibility but fail to shift the narrative (symbolic) or engage platforms that mediate attention (informational). Conversely, an initiative that only exists online without grounding in real-world actions or infrastructures may become noise, not signal. True impact arises when levers are pulled in harmony: when symbolic clarity, narrative control, digital distribution, and material disruption are synchronized.

This requires not just awareness but *tools*—ways to diagnose, visualize, and track obscured dynamics as they unfold. One approach is the development of **composite indices**: analytical frameworks that combine disparate signals across domains. For instance, a geopolitical stability index might blend military deployments (physical), press freedom metrics (informational), religious or nationalist rhetoric (symbolic), and demographic pressure points (emergent stress). No single data point tells the whole story. But when layered and contextualized, patterns emerge—patterns that allow for proactive movement rather than reactive paralysis.

Similarly, **network mapping** can expose the architecture of influence. In a corporate context, this might involve identifying not just formal leadership, but informal brokers of information—those who connect departments, whisper in decision-makers' ears, or hold the trust of dissenting voices. In a cultural context, mapping the spread of symbols, memes, and narratives can reveal which nodes serve as amplifiers or suppressors of change. Network theory teaches us that power is not always at the center; sometimes it lies at the edges, in the hands of those who bridge disconnected clusters or control the gates of visibility.

Yet building diagnostic tools is only one part of the equation. The harder task is to **interpret the signals** without being overwhelmed by them. The modern world is not short on data. It is drowning in it. But data without discernment becomes noise. Discernment begins with asking the right questions: What layer does this phenomenon inhabit? What are its upstream and downstream effects? Which myths does it draw upon? What power structures reinforce or resist it? Where is the leverage point?

Leverage points—those critical nodes where a small shift triggers outsized consequences—are rarely obvious. They are often hidden beneath surface symptoms, protected by institutional inertia or ideological framing. Sometimes the leverage point is a law. Sometimes it's a symbol. Sometimes it's a piece of infrastructure so ubiquitous that we forget to notice it. Mastery involves developing the sensitivity to see these fault lines before they fracture.

There is also a **temporal** dimension to mastery. Systems evolve. What is obscure today may become obvious tomorrow. A protest becomes a revolution. A tweet becomes a movement. A fringe idea becomes orthodoxy. Timing matters—not just in action, but in observation. To engage effectively, one must sense the rhythm of unfolding change, the signals that precede tipping points, the quiet convergences that culminate in sudden upheaval.

This is why **strategic patience** is often more valuable than speed. The master of the obscured is not always the first to act, but the first to *understand*. They operate from a state of deliberate attentiveness, cultivating perspectives that extend beyond the moment. They watch patterns, test assumptions, simulate consequences. They resist the pull of reactive acceleration in favor of calibrated intervention.

And yet, mastery is not omniscience. It is not the illusion of control, but the cultivation of capacity. To master the obscured is to know that the map is not the territory, that systems surprise, that narratives rupture, and that entropy always lurks. But it is also to know that clarity is possible—that with the right lens, even the most chaotic surface can reveal an underlying logic.

In that spirit, synthesis is not merely academic. It is practical. It is not an abstract model to admire, but a working lens to navigate complexity. It can be applied to organizational strategy, personal development, political engagement, or cultural transformation. It helps us diagnose not only what is happening, but why—and what to do about it.

We now stand at a threshold. The previous chapters have offered fragments—histories, mechanisms, principles, and anomalies. This chapter does not tie them into a neat bow. It threads them into a **living system**—a toolkit, a compass, a set of coordinates. It invites the reader to step not just into knowledge, but into strategy. Not just into observation, but into orchestration.

Mastery of the obscured is not domination. It is **discernment with responsibility**. For to see what others cannot is to bear a burden—to act not from arrogance, but from a deeper ethic of care. In a world where systems shape lives, where beliefs can be weaponized, and where the invisible dictates the visible, what we do with our understanding matters. How we wield it, how we share it, and how we respond to it defines whether we replicate the old architectures of control—or build new frameworks of possibility.

Because ultimately, the obscured principles are not just about systems. They are about *us*. Our minds, our myths, our models, our movements. To master them is not to escape the world, but to engage it more skillfully, more consciously, and more creatively. That is the challenge. That is the promise. And that is the next chapter—written not in this book, but in the choices we make beyond it.

10.1 Ethical Harnessing

Understanding the hidden architecture of systems grants a kind of power—quiet, far-reaching, often invisible. But with such knowledge comes a question that is as old as philosophy itself: what will you *do* with it? The mastery of obscured principles is not a neutral skillset. It confers the ability to alter outcomes, shape perceptions, influence decisions, and redirect trajectories. Used carelessly, it becomes manipulation. Used wisely, it becomes design. Used self-servingly, it becomes control. Used ethically, it becomes stewardship.

There is a fundamental difference between *knowing* the levers of power and *wielding* them with care. Many of the world's greatest harms have come not from ignorance, but from partial understanding deployed without constraint—tools of influence used in the absence of moral clarity. The twentieth century gave us propaganda machines, total surveillance, and psychological conditioning experiments that demonstrated just how far systems could shape human behavior when unmoored from ethics. Today, we face similar temptations, but at a much more granular scale.

The digital tools we've built—algorithms, platforms, predictive analytics, nudges—are not merely passive infrastructures. They are **architectures of choice**. They decide what is seen and unseen, what is amplified and obscured, what is remembered and forgotten. Whoever controls them has the ability to direct society's emotional and cognitive energy. This does not require force. It requires framing. And this is precisely why the ethical dimension cannot be deferred to engineers, lawyers, or regulators alone. It must be internalized by anyone who seeks to work with these systems.

Ethical harnessing begins with the **recognition of asymmetry**. The power to shape narratives, influence networks, or nudge decisions is not evenly distributed. Some individuals and institutions hold more keys, more access, more leverage. The first ethical responsibility, then, is to examine one's own position within this matrix. What do you have access to? What can you affect? Who cannot? And how will your actions ripple outward through the social, informational, and symbolic layers?

Transparency is the first safeguard. Not radical openness—some systems must protect privacy, security, and creative process—but intelligibility. People must understand the basic contours of the systems they interact with. They must know when they are being nudged, tracked, ranked, or categorized. They must have the right to challenge these systems, to understand the logic behind decisions that affect them, and to appeal unjust outcomes. Without this, trust degrades, and systems calcify into silent coercion.

Accountability is the second safeguard. Designers, engineers, leaders, and communicators must not hide behind the complexity of their tools. "The algorithm did it" is not a defense; it is a deflection. Every system reflects choices—what to include, what to weigh, what to ignore. These choices embed values. And values must be confronted openly. Accountability means that when harm occurs—bias in a hiring algorithm, disinformation spread by a recommender engine, or manipulation in a political campaign—there is a clear chain of responsibility. Without this, feedback loops become toxic and irreversible.

Inclusive design is the third. Systems built for the powerful tend to reinforce power. Systems built with diverse inputs tend to serve broader interests. This means involving affected communities in the design of tools that will shape their lives. It means testing assumptions across cultural, socioeconomic, and cognitive differences. It means refusing to confuse the "average user" with the "right user." It is slow, often messy work—but it is the only path to legitimacy in systems that claim to serve publics.

And yet, even these safeguards are not enough. The world is too complex for fixed ethical rules. This is why **scenario ethics** must become part of any responsible strategy. Scenario ethics is the practice of stress-testing one's values under different conditions. What if your system is used in a warzone? What if it is co-opted by an authoritarian regime? What if it scales faster than expected, or reaches unintended audiences? These are not edge cases. They are inevitabilities in a hyperconnected world. The question is not whether the system can be misused, but how you will respond when it is.

Ethical harnessing does not mean avoiding influence. It means becoming *conscious* of it. Influence is not inherently wrong. It is the basis of leadership, education, art, and even friendship. What matters is whether it is rooted in truth, proportionality, and the dignity of those affected. To manipulate is to impose. To guide with consent is to empower.

In mastering the obscured, one gains not a license to dominate, but a **duty to discern**. The systems we touch affect lives, cultures, futures. They are not toys. They are extensions of human will, and they will reflect either our fears or our aspirations. The line between exploitation and elevation lies not in the code, but in the conscience.

And so, ethical harnessing becomes the bridge between understanding and action. It asks not only what is possible, but what is *right*. It reframes mastery as service, power as responsibility, and systems as stories we write together—whether with algorithms or with words, with institutions or with rituals.

10.2 Actionable Playbooks

All theory, no matter how elegant, remains inert without practice. Having mapped the hidden architectures and committed to ethical engagement, we now arrive at a final demand: action. What do we *do* with this knowledge—concretely, repeatedly, sustainably? What does it mean to operationalize mastery? The answer lies in creating **playbooks**—structured, iterative paths of action tailored to different agents: individuals, organizations, and states.

At the individual level, the goal is not to overhaul society overnight, but to embed **pattern recognition** and systemic thinking into daily decisions. This means developing the capacity to spot leverage points—where a single question, habit, or message can produce cascading effects. For example, understanding how media flows shape perceptions may inform how and what you choose to share. Recognizing symbolic triggers may shift the metaphors you use in storytelling, teaching, or marketing. Even small shifts—asking better questions in meetings, reframing problems to colleagues, questioning defaults—accumulate over time into new cultural norms.

But action requires structure. A personal playbook might begin with **diagnosis**: what systems am I part of? What stories do I reinforce? Where does my influence lie? Then comes **intervention**: choose one layer—informational, symbolic, relational—and test a small shift. Observe the effects. **Reflect.** Then adapt. This is **rapid prototyping** at the micro-level: experiments in perception, conversation, and behavior that iterate toward better alignment with principle and purpose.

Organizations—whether businesses, nonprofits, or movements—require a broader set of tools. The first step is **systems mapping**: charting not just workflows or hierarchies, but cultural beliefs, informal power brokers, feedback loops, and mythologies. Every organization has stories it tells itself. Some are empowering. Others are obsolete. Mapping these invisible forces allows for targeted shifts that reshape not only processes, but paradigms.

Once mapped, organizations must engage in **iterative cycles**: design a new process, product, or policy; prototype at small scale; measure emergent effects across all three layers—physical, informational, symbolic. Was a new onboarding system merely efficient, or did it signal care? Did a marketing campaign merely gain clicks, or alter public sentiment? The goal is to evolve not just outputs, but identity.

Crucially, organizations must invest in **learning infrastructures**. This means turning every decision into a feedback loop, every failure into a case study, and every success into a replicable pattern. Too often, institutions reward execution without introspection. But sustainable mastery requires continuous adaptation. That means dedicated time for retrospective analysis, cross-functional synthesis, and cultural digestion. The question is not just "Did it work?" but "What did it teach us about the system?"

States and institutions face a more complex task. Their scale makes agility difficult, and their mandate makes ethics essential. Their playbooks must begin with **diagnostic indices**—composite tools that track systemic health across layers. A state cannot govern well if it monitors only GDP and crime rates. It must also track trust in institutions, media literacy, symbolic polarization, infrastructural resilience, and predictive stress signals. These indices become the dashboards of modern governance—not as ends in themselves, but as guides for prioritization and foresight.

From there, governments can deploy **strategic foresight units**—cross-disciplinary teams that simulate future scenarios, test policy assumptions, and design **early-warning systems**. These are not utopian projects. They are essential in a world of accelerating change. Pandemic response, digital sovereignty, climate resilience, AI regulation—none of these challenges can be addressed reactively. States must shift from bureaucratic routines to living playbooks that learn, adapt, and coordinate across sectors.

Across all levels, from individual to institutional, one principle remains: **embed continuous learning loops**. The world is too dynamic for static playbooks. What worked last year may be obsolete tomorrow. Mastery requires humility: the willingness to revisit assumptions, retire sacred cows, and evolve faster than the system you are trying to navigate.

This demands **time architecture**. Most systems are built around short-term metrics. But real impact requires dual tracking—operating at the pace of now while designing for the future. This is the discipline of **strategic patience**: moving quickly in execution, but slowly in reflection. Rushing creates fragility. Pausing creates resilience.

The ultimate goal of these playbooks is not merely to intervene in the system, but to change how the system **sees itself**. This is where transformation becomes generative. When a school sees itself not as a factory of credentials but as an incubator of symbolic literacy. When a company sees its supply chain not as a cost center but as a cultural actor. When a citizen sees their vote not as a ritual but as a symbolic act of power. Then the system begins to awaken to its own architecture—and redesign itself from within.

That is the final act of synthesis: not control, but **co-creation**. Not rigid rules, but living frameworks. Not isolated genius, but distributed insight. Mastery of the obscured is not about seeing behind the curtain. It is about redesigning the stage.

Because in the end, every system is human-made. And every human has the potential to make new systems. The question is whether we will do so passively—or with eyes open, principles clear, and tools in hand.

Conclusion

"The God of peace will soon crush Satan under your feet." — Romans 16:20

The obscured is no longer obscure. By now, the architecture has been sketched, the mechanisms revealed, the patterns named. What was once ambient and elusive—the silent blueprints behind power, perception, and progress—has been drawn into light. And yet, if this book has done its work well, it has not left you with a sense of finality. It has opened a door.

We began not with prophecy, but with perception. Not by seeking new horizons, but by learning to see the ones we already inhabit with new clarity. The real transformation does not lie in acquiring secret knowledge or becoming fluent in esoteric terminology. It lies in cultivating a new mode of attention—a disciplined, discerning way of seeing the world and ourselves within it. To know the obscured principles is not to memorize them. It is to live in relationship with them.

At its core, this has never been a book about conspiracy, domination, or paranoia. It is a book about *conscious design*. A book about how systems, symbols, identities, and infrastructures converge to shape lived reality—quietly, persistently, often invisibly. It is also a book about the invitation to participate in that shaping process. Not as masters of the world, but as mindful stewards of its unfolding. Because every system, no matter how vast or ancient, was built. And what is built can be rebuilt.

You have now encountered the contours of archetypal frameworks and learned how deeply they echo through our myths, institutions, and brands. You have examined the layered nature of reality—how cities, symbols, and algorithms interlace to define what feels real. You have seen how emergence arises not from force, but from interaction, feedback, and scale. You've touched the threads of hidden power hierarchies, media ecologies, and symbolic warfare. You've stepped into the domain of economic engines, memetic contagion, predictive futures, and cognitive scripts.

And then, you were invited to synthesize.

But knowledge without ethics is brittle. So we paused. We asked: What is the responsibility of seeing clearly? What happens when you become fluent in the structures others move through blindly? This is where mastery transforms into stewardship. Where seeing the invisible does not license manipulation, but demands deeper moral rigor. Power—real power—is not simply the ability to act. It is the wisdom to choose not to.

And so, we grounded our insights in playbooks—practical paths for activating understanding. Whether you are an individual trying to influence your immediate ecosystem, an organization aiming to shift culture, or a state navigating geopolitical complexity, the final invitation is the same: embed learning. Honor context. Iterate with intention. And build systems that do not merely function—but evolve.

Still, there is one final truth worth holding close: even the most obscured principles are not immutable. They, too, are patterns— patterns written by human hands, shaped by human fears, sustained by human habits. And that means they are subject to change. No architecture is permanent. No narrative is unshakable. The myth of inevitability is one of the most powerful illusions in history. But once you've seen the blueprint, it loses its hold.

The Obscured Principles

You now possess something rare—not certainty, but orientation. Not a script, but a compass. The obscured principles are no longer hidden from you. They have been named, traced, held up to the light. And in doing so, they have become tools—not for control, but for consciousness.

As you close this book, you do not return to the same world you entered. You return equipped—with new eyes, new language, and a deeper sense that the future is not something to predict, but something to shape. Quietly. Courageously. Intentionally.

Not with dominance, but with design.

Not with fear, but with clarity.

Not with noise, but with presence.

Because the obscured is never just out there.

It is also in here—woven into thought, attention, and will.

And now, you see.

www.ingramcontent.com/pod-product-compliance
Lightning Source LLC
Chambersburg PA
CBHW060358090426
42734CB00011B/2173